Ayrshire

40 Coast and Country Walks

The author and publisher have made every effort to ensure that the information in this publication is accurate, and accept no responsibility whatsoever for any loss, injury or inconvenience experienced by any person or persons whilst using this book.

published by
pocket mountains ltd
Holm Street, Moffat,
Dumfries and Galloway
pocketmountains.com

ISBN: 978-1-9070253-9-6

Text and photography copyright © Phil Turner

The right of Phil Turner to be identified as the Author of this work has been asserted by him in accordance with the Copyright, Designs and Patents Act 1988

A catalogue record for this book is available from the British Library

Contains Ordnance Survey data © Crown copyright and database right 2014, supported by out of copyright mapping from 1945-1961

Printed in Poland REP2016

Introduction

One of Scotland's most fertile regions, Ayrshire has it all – from beach to pasture, hill to forest, all interspersed with echoes of an industrial past. Shoreside fields produce some of the finest early potatoes around, and clifftop pastures are home to herds of Ayrshire cattle producing excellent meat as well as the key ingredient in the famous Dunlop cheese. Once the domain of Covenanters and latterly heavy industry, outdoor pursuits – including golf at several world-class courses – now draw visitors into the countryside that inspired Robert Burns.

This guide contains forty moderate walks which offer surprising variety, from sedate strolls along sandy beaches to rough heather moorland and hillwalks. Most routes begin and end at a town or village with public transport options and welcoming accommodation to enable a thorough exploration of the surrounding countryside.

The routes in this book are divided into four sections, each of which is introduced by a summary giving an overview of the area and a map showing the start point of each walk.

History

Beneath the quiet rolling farmland of Ayrshire lies a turbulent past, with vitrified hillforts, Viking invasions, William Wallace, Robert the Bruce and the relentless and bloody pursuit of Covenanters seeking sanctuary in the hills and woods of the county. Many of the walks in this guide follow in the footsteps of earls and kings, painters and poets.

Prehistoric remains such as the Dagon Stone in Darvel and the cup and ring markings beneath the Ballochmyle Viaduct in Mauchline, along with whisperings of Druidic activity, point to early habitation in the area, but permanent settlement seems to have coincided with the introduction of Christianity by St Ninian in 397AD.

Scottish patriot William Wallace had many family connections in Ayrshire and Barr Castle in the town of Galston was reputed to have hosted Wallace and his men as they evaded English troops. According to legend he escaped a siege of the castle by climbing down the branches of a nearby overhanging tree. Wallace invented a kind of handball game played against the castle walls in order to keep his men fit, and this unique game was played in the area until the mid-20th century.

Robert the Bruce was probably born in Turnberry Castle, and went on to carry out numerous guerilla raids against the English in the area. Several years before his triumph at Bannockburn in 1314 he employed the same tactics to win a battle at Loudoun Hill near Darvel.

The area is dotted with evidence of the rule of the barons in the 13th to 15th centuries – particularly Clan Kennedy, self-proclaimed 'Kings of Carrick' – who erected a series of castles and peel towers in South Ayrshire. These families exerted significant influence over the population, acting as judge and jury; the Dule Trees located on their estates served as gallows and as symbols of their authority. Later grand castles such as Culzean near Maybole remain as reminders of the Kennedys' influence over the region.

In the late 17th century the Covenanters, a Scottish Presbyterian movement resistant to the religious observance imposed by James II and then Charles II, held secret services known as conventicles in the Ayrshire countryside on pain of death if discovered by government forces. Many Covenanters were executed where they stood if they refused to swear allegiance to the King, and there are numerous memorial stones to these martyrs dotted throughout the Ayrshire hills.

Textile manufacture dominated the industrial landscape of 18th- and 19th-century Ayrshire, with the Irvine Valley, in particular, renowned for a lace industry initiated by immigrant Huguenot weavers. Coal mining and iron smelting was also a big employer in the area and coal from Ayrshire's opencast mines still makes up much of the UK's total output.

In modern times heavy industry has declined in the region, and several walks in this guide cut through the countryside on former railway tracks which fell out of use as the economic landscape altered. While some substantial plants and factories have withdrawn, the Scottish aviation industry remains centred around Glasgow Prestwick International Airport north of Ayr, famous as the only place in Britain visited by Elvis Presley on his way back from military service in 1960.

Today the rural southern part of Ayrshire is the agricultural heartland of Scotland, with potatoes grown by the coast and Ayrshire cattle famed worldwide for their milk and beef. Ayrshire pork products can be found on the tables of Michelin-starred restaurants throughout the UK.

As the birthplace of Robert Burns, Ayrshire features heavily in the Bard's works, especially the small town of Alloway which attracts many visitors drawn to the Robert Burns Birthplace Museum and locations from the popular poem *Tam o' Shanter*.

Wildlife

Due to a diverse range of habitats, Ayrshire is home to a surprising variety of flora and fauna. There are many Sites of Special Scientific Interest (SSSI), from the mudflats and saltmarshes of the Irvine Estuary to the Muirkirk moorland which supports a population of hen harriers and short-eared owls.

Many of the walks featured here pass through some of the finest native woodland in Scotland, particularly in river valleys such as the River Ayr Gorge in Failford – a steep ravine containing oak, ash and larch and invertebrates, plants, bats and fungi. Bright kingfishers and bobbing dippers can be seen perched on riverside rocks as the unmistakable sound of the great spotted woodpecker echoes through the forest and red squirrels leap from tree to tree. At dusk noctule and Daubenton's bats perform a valuable service in their search for midges. Ayrshire's woodlands are something special.

The local nature reserve of Catrine Voes in East Ayrshire is a good location to view the Atlantic salmon run in spring and autumn, as well as trout, eels and mammals such as otters and water voles.

Coastal walkers may be lucky enough to spot the fin of a basking shark moving slowly offshore, seemingly unperturbed by the gannets from the large colony on Ailsa Craig plunging into the sea from unfeasible heights. The coastal mudflats are a valuable habitat for wading birds such as oystercatchers and greenshank, and the distinctive 'computer game' call of the lapwing is a common accompaniment to walks in Ayrshire.

Safety

Although moderate, many of these walks are on unmarked paths and faint tracks that are rough underfoot. Appropriate footwear should be selected based on the route description and weather forecasts. The sketch maps provided are planning aids that should be supplemented with more detailed mapping, such as that by the Ordnance Survey. A few OS maps will be required to cover the whole county – check the information panel at the beginning of each walk.

The weather on the west coast of Scotland is notoriously unpredictable and even a short walk can quickly become a major epic when the conditions change – with that in mind it is important to pack wind- and waterproof clothing and adequate warm layers to allow the walk to be completed no matter what the weather.

Many of the walks are suitable for accompanied children – some are even pushchair accessible – but a few are more suited to experienced walkers and judgement should be exercised.

Access

Most of Ayrshire is served by an excellent bus network, with the coastal A77 to the port at Stranraer particularly convenient for walkers completing stages of the Ayrshire Coastal Path. Of the walk start points in this guide, all but the most rural settlement is provided with a bus link to the nearest town, and the Glasgow to Stranraer railway runs through the county making numerous stops. Ayr forms a natural transport hub and makes a good base for exploring the area. The Traveline Scotland website is a useful planning tool (travelinescotland.com).

The Isle of Arran can be accessed by ferry from Ardrossan in North Ayrshire and Great Cumbrae is linked to Largs by a regular ferry making the short journey across the Fairlie Roads.

The Land Reform (Scotland) Act 2003 gave walkers rights of access over most of Scotland away from residential buildings, but these rights must be exercised responsibly and the Scottish Outdoor Access Code followed at all times in order to maintain cordial relationships with landowners. As much of Ayrshire is farmland, walkers should pay particular attention when crossing fields containing livestock, especially if accompanied by a dog (outdooraccess-scotland.com).

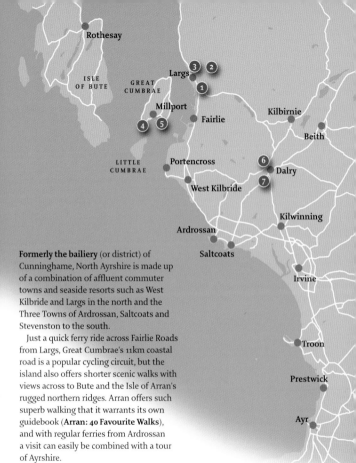

Formerly the bailiery (or district) of Cunninghame, North Ayrshire is made up of a combination of affluent commuter towns and seaside resorts such as West Kilbride and Largs in the north and the Three Towns of Ardrossan, Saltcoats and Stevenston to the south.

Just a quick ferry ride across Fairlie Roads from Largs, Great Cumbrae's 11km coastal road is a popular cycling circuit, but the island also offers shorter scenic walks with views across to Bute and the Isle of Arran's rugged northern ridges. Arran offers such superb walking that it warrants its own guidebook (**Arran: 40 Favourite Walks**), and with regular ferries from Ardrossan a visit can easily be combined with a tour of Ayrshire.

Great Cumbrae is explored in two walks in this chapter while the seafront at Largs is the start point for two further routes – one a bracing hike to a viewpoint above the town, the other tackling an Iron Age hillfort on a branch of the Ayrshire Coastal Path. A third short expedition from Largs makes a scenic waterfall its objective. To the south, Dalry is the setting off point for two walks that explore the countryside and rivers surrounding this typical inland Ayrshire market town.

6

North Ayrshire

Douglas Park and Castle Hill

Distance 5.4km **Time** 2 hours
Terrain a mix of pavement, beaten earth
and grassy paths which can be boggy in
places; final steep ascent with steps
Map OS Explorer 341 **Access** Largs is well
served by bus and rail, with regular trains
to Glasgow

An out-and-back walk through parkland
with a bracing ascent to a rocky viewpoint
high above Largs. Near the viewpoint are
the remains of an Iron Age hillfort, whilst
a 5000-year-old chambered cairn can be
visited on the way.

From the car park opposite Nardini's
Restaurant in Largs head south along the
promenade, passing the ferry terminal and
amusement arcades and crossing the Gogo
Water at the bridge opposite the
Benedictine Monastery. Continue along

the front until the intersection with May
Street. You could detour ahead to visit the
21m-high Battle of Largs Monument, or
'The Pencil' as it is known locally, which
commemorates the Battle of Largs in 1263
between Scotland and Norway over control
of the western seaboard. The battle ended
in stalemate but it marked the beginning
of the end of Viking power in Scotland,
culminating in the 1266 Treaty of Perth
when the Hebrides and Isle of Man were
ceded to Scotland from Norway while
Norway's ownership of Shetland and
Orkney were confirmed. It wasn't until the
marriage agreement between King James
III and Margaret of Denmark (and Norway)
in 1468 that Orkney and Shetland came
back under Scottish control.

From the top of May Street walk away
from the sea, turning left into Anderson

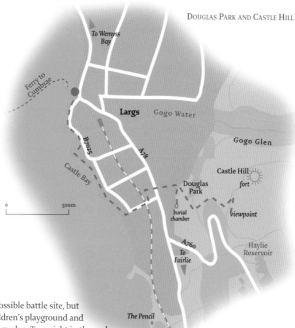

Park – a possible battle site, but now a children's playground and memorial garden. Turn right in the park to emerge onto the main road.

Cross this carefully into Douglas Park opposite, neatly manicured with tennis courts and bowling greens. Following the avenue as it curves right, you'll see a gate in the fence. Before going through the gate, detour along the avenue around the right-hand bend to visit the Haylie Chambered Tomb; only the innermost chamber remains, but it is 3000 years old. Return to the gate and pass through it to begin your ascent.

The path varies from well-constructed railway-sleeper steps to wide grassy tracks – regardless of the surface the angle of ascent is fairly steep, giving plenty of opportunity to pause, turn around and take in the views over the Clyde. Cross a farm track part way up. The final ascent is up a long set of steps. Upon reaching the top, turn south to reach a view indicator and superb panoramic views. Over to the northeast is Castle Hill – a rocky outcrop and the remains of an Iron Age fort with evidence of a ditch and low rampart.

The return walk is the same way, back to the top of the steps and down the hill – this time with the Cumbraes and the Clyde spread out in front of you.

◀ Largs, Great Cumbrae and Bute from Castle Hill

Greeto Falls and Bridge

Distance 5km **Time** 2 hours
Terrain a mix of road, grassy paths and almost trackless moorland; all can be boggy in places; one stile to cross; rough ascent to radio mast **Map** OS Explorer 341 **Access** Largs seafront is a 1km walk away; alternatively, there is a small car park by the former Flatt Farm site

This linear walk from Largs leads you high above the Gogo Water to the popular picnicking and wild swimming spot of Greeto Falls, or 'the Gretas' as the locals call them. There are also options to extend your walk over more challenging ground.

It's a straightforward 1km walk from Largs promenade up Gateside Street and onto Flatt Road, passing Largs Academy and continuing along Bellesdale Avenue. Alternatively, from the car park at the former site of Flatt Farm, take the steep metalled road up the hill towards the various telecommunication masts, pausing to look back at the views across to the Cumbraes, the Clyde and beyond. Pass through the gate to reach the grassy path high above the heavily wooded Gogo Glen and follow this easy trail for 1.5km to reach the bridge and falls. In the summer months local children jump from various heights on the adjacent cliffs into the pool known as the Cat's Eye – not recommended, of course, but a good way to cool off on a hot day!

The hills ahead form part of Clyde Muirshiel Regional Park – the largest Regional Park in Scotland, with some excellent largely-pathless and remote walking. Suitably equipped hillwalkers can experience this challenging terrain by

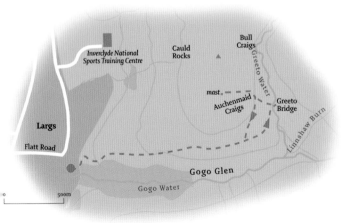

◀ The Gogo Water cutting through the hills of Clyde Muirshiel Regional Park

crossing Greeto Bridge and traversing the slope before crossing Linnshaw Burn as the path begins to peter out. Descend steeply to a bridge over the Gogo Water and scramble up the other side onto the open, pathless terrain below Rigging Hill before curving west to Castle Hill and descending via Douglas Park (*see page 8*).

Otherwise, after a pause to admire the steep-sided, rocky waterfalls, navigationally-confident and appropriately-shod walkers can follow a faint path (non-existent in places) north over rough ground before curving around to the west to reach the old

mast above Auchenmaid Craigs. The views across to the North Ayrshire hills and the Clyde are spectacular, so spend some time wandering around the area before beginning your descent.

From the mast, head back the way you came before cutting the corner to pick up the main path back to the car park.

Retrace your steps whilst watching the ferries make their frequent crossings to and from Great Cumbrae. Look out for the local landmark of Cockmalane Cottage visible across the glen, nestled in the northwestern slope of Castle Hill.

Knock Hill

Distance 13km **Time** 4 hours **Terrain** a mix of roads, earth and grassy paths; very boggy in places; spiralling ascent to summit **Map** OS Explorer 341 **Access** Largs is well served by bus and rail, with regular trains to Glasgow

Enjoy spectacular views over Largs and the Clyde on this circular hill walk.

From the car park opposite Nardini's in Largs, head north along the promenade, passing the RNLI lifeboat station and Vikingar on the right, before reaching the Noddsdale Water and turning inland. The route follows the Ayrshire Coastal Path, and the green waymarks will accompany you for the majority of the walk, indicating any changes in direction. Follow the

footpath to reach the A78, turning right and then left to enter Barr Crescent. As soon as possible, take the waymarked footpath on the left running alongside the burn and follow the water until you come to Brisbane Glen Road.

Turn left and follow the road, initially on pavement but then on the road itself as open countryside is reached. Be careful of cars on this section. Keep an eye open for the track to Brisbane Mains Farm on the left – again it is well waymarked, but easy to miss if focused on the countryside unfurling as the road leaves civilisation. Take this path as it gently climbs the hillside, pass through the farmyard, avoiding the free-range hens, and strike out along the muddy farm track. This is a

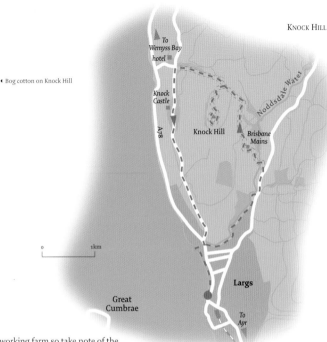

◀ Bog cotton on Knock Hill

To Wemyss Bay hotel

Knock Castle

A78

Knock Hill

Brisbane Mains

Noddsdale Water

Largs

To Ayr

Great Cumbrae

0   1km

working farm so take note of the farmer's instructions regarding gates and minor diversions as you go.

As the angle of ascent increases the path becomes less defined and more boggy. Take the left waymarked fork at the end of a small copse to bear northwest along an open grassy track. At another fork, remain on the main path to begin the approach to the hillfort and trig point. As the path spirals up the hill, the Cumbrae islands and the Clyde come into view, a taster of the 360-degree panorama that meets you at the summit. Drop back down by the same route to the path junction, go left and begin your descent towards Blackhouse Burn.

Follow the path through potentially muddy farmland, ignoring the path branching off to the left, to enter a small wooded area. Upon reaching the metalled road by Manor Park Hotel, turn left to follow this quiet single-carriageway road south, passing the privately owned Knock Castle and Routenburn Golf Course whilst marvelling at the great views across the Clyde.

Eventually you reach the main A78. After crossing the bridge over the Noddsdale Water, turn right to retrace your steps along the promenade to the car park.

Fintry Bay on Great Cumbrae

Distance 7.9km **Time** 3 hours
Terrain pavements, country lanes, earth
footpaths and grassy tracks; boggy in
places; gradual ascent and short, sharp
descent to Fintry Bay **Map** OS Explorer 341
Access ferry to Cumbrae Slip and
connecting bus to Millport Old Pier

**An idyllic walk where minimal effort is
rewarded by fine views across Bute and the
Firth of Clyde to the rocky North Arran hills.**

Great Cumbrae Island is easily accessible
from Largs thanks to a regular shuttle ferry
service which runs at 15-minute intervals
in the summer months and 30 minutes in
winter. A bus meets the ferry at Cumbrae
Slip and conveys passengers the 7km to
Millport. Get off at the last stop – the Old
Pier by the Royal George Hotel.

Cross the road and head up Cardiff
Street, forking right onto Golf Road which
heads towards Millport Golf Club. This
quiet country road rises gently, passing the
three farms at Kirkton, with the island's
original cemetery – the oldest gravestone

dating back to 1703 – located between Mid
Kirkton Farm and a caravan park and
accessed via a decorative gate and turnstile.
Further along the road you'll pass the
modern replacement on the right, in use
since the 1930s.

Before reaching the golf club car park fork
left as indicated by the green 'Isle of
Cumbrae Walks' signpost and curve left
onto a farm track, passing a series of white-
washed farm buildings. The track becomes
unsurfaced before reaching a waymarked
kissing gate – go through this and follow
the grassy track as it curves right, then left
to climb to the top of the hill. From here,
expect spectacular views across to Kilchattan
Bay on Bute, with Mount Stuart – residence
of the Marquess of Bute – visible further
north on the wooded hillside.

Continue along the track – which can be
muddy after rain – with Ben Lomond and
the Loch Lomond hills on the horizon
ahead. Go through a kissing gate and watch

for the Gowk Stane slightly downhill on the left. This is one of several such stones in Scotland, with the name meaning 'stone of the cuckoo' or 'fool' in Scots. From here the views over Bute are supplemented by the rocky ridge of the North Arran hills, with a profile claimed to represent a 'Sleeping Warrior'. The grassy path begins to slope downhill – quite steeply in places – before entering a patch of woodland and emerging at the surfaced road.

Turn right along this quiet road to reach Fintry Bay and tearoom, a popular stop for cyclists completing the circular route around the island and those that fancy a picnic on the red sandy beach. Turn around and head back along the road – there is a pavement, but traffic is very light. Pass a war memorial overlooking the sea and the shallow bay at Sheriff's Port. Here, an iron kissing gate on the left-hand side of the road offers a path back to the outward route at Kirkton, but carry on along the road instead. Shortly after a rocky picnic area above the beach, look for a green 'Isle of Cumbrae Walks' sign on the right indicating a narrow footpath.

Follow the path – faint in places – as it winds along the rocky shoreline and across a series of improvised bridges to reach a field. Head slightly inland whilst continuing to shadow the shoreline, and go through a gate alongside a water treatment plant. Follow the vehicle track towards the boatyard and pass through a gate to rejoin the road. Turn right and follow the road back into Millport, passing a row of impressive villas before turning right to follow Millburn, Crichton, Miller and Clyde Streets back to the start.

◀ The Gowk Stane with Bute and Arran beyond

Millport and Farland Point

Distance 6.3km including cathedral loop
Time 2 hours 30 **Terrain** pavements and
good footpaths; largely flat; cathedral
detour involves steps, but can be avoided
Map OS Explorer 341 **Access** ferry to
Cumbrae Slip and connecting bus to
Millport Old Pier

**With good paths throughout, this is an
accessible walk which offers pleasing
views across Millport Bay and the wider
Firth of Clyde.**

Great Cumbrae Island is easily accessible
from Largs by shuttle ferry. A bus meets
the ferry at Cumbrae Slip and conveys
passengers the 7km to Millport. Get off at
the last stop – the Old Pier by the Royal
George Hotel.

Start to retrace the bus route by
following the promenade past the old
harbour and the varied shops overlooking
the bay – including The Wedge, Britain's
narrowest house which is barely wide
enough to accommodate the front door.
Pass Garrison House, built in 1745 to house
the captain and officers of the Revenue
Cutter *Royal George* stationed in Millport.
Following a fire in 2001 and subsequent
dereliction, the building has just reopened
as a community hub, including a GP
surgery, council offices and library. Turn
left along College Street immediately after
Garrison House to head towards The
Cathedral of The Isles. There are numerous
steps after this point, so this short detour
can easily be omitted.

Climbing uphill along College Street,
pass Our Lady of Perpetual Succour before
coming to the walled, wooded grounds of
The Cathedral of The Isles on the right.
Follow the tree-lined avenue and ascend
the steps to enter the building. The

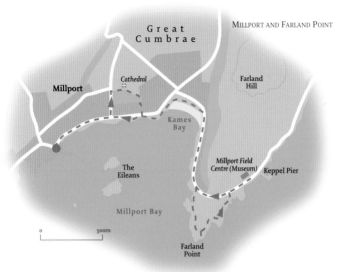

Millport

Cathedral

Farland
Hill

Kames
Bay

The
Eileans

Millport Field
Centre (Museum)   Keppel Pier

Millport Bay

0   500m

Farland
Point

smallest cathedral in Britain, it dates from
1851 when it was built as a theological
college for the Scottish Episcopal Church.
Pass the main cathedral building and the
former college buildings (now a retreat
centre) to the rear and leave the cathedral
grounds via the eastern entrance. Drop
back down to the seafront and continue
east (left) along the promenade.

Skirt round Kames Bay with its sandy
beach and follow the pavement below the
cliffs of Farland Hill. On the right after
500m a wooden kissing gate sits alongside
a larger gate (accessible if you have a Radar
Lock key), leading to a pleasant and well-
made footpath through scrubland.

Follow the path around to rocky Farland
Point which offers views back across
Millport Bay as well as south down the
Firth of Clyde. The cliffs of Little Cumbrae
Island (or 'Wee Cumbrae') are clearly

visible across The Tan with the rocky
ridgeline forming Arran's Sleeping Warrior
beyond on the horizon. Across to the
Ayrshire mainland, you can see the section
of coastline that makes up the Portencross
to Largs Marina leg of the Ayrshire Coastal
Path, notably the buildings of Hunterston
Nuclear Power Station and the cranes and
coal conveyors of the Deep Water Terminal.

The footpath eventually re-emerges at
the coast road. Turn right to reach the
Millport Field Centre at Keppel Pier, which
houses an aquarium and museum.

Turn around and retrace your steps past
the boulder forming a memorial to the
Scottish National Antarctic Expedition of
1902-1904 which, on returning, made its
first Scottish landing in Millport. Continue
along the coast road to return to Millport,
making sure you look out for the painted
Crocodile Rock in the bay.

◀ Millport from Farland Point

Doggartland and Dalry

Distance 4.3km **Time** 1 hour 30
Terrain good earth footpaths, pavements
and surfaced roads; muddy sections;
gentle ascent **Map** OS Explorer 333
Access trains from Glasgow and Stranraer
to Dalry; buses between Glasgow and
Ardrossan call at Dalry

**A quiet circular walk with literary
connections across farmland and on
country roads on the outskirts of Dalry.**

There is parking at The Cross in the
centre of Dalry, a popular meeting place
overshadowed by Dalry Trinity Church
and St Margaret's Church, or in one of the
free car parks in the surrounding streets.
Walk along North Street before turning
right onto the main B780 Kilbirnie road.
Keep to the pavement as the road heads
out of town. Before it crosses the Rye
Water, turn left along a footpath beside
a derelict factory.

This path passes the rear of the factory
to reach a junction of trails. The main
path bears left towards Ryefield House,
another continues straight ahead to
Ryefield Stables, and a short waymarker
post inscribed 'Doggartland Walk' indicates
a leafy footpath shadowing the Rye Water,
while a bolted doorway in the wall on the
right provides a glimpse of a beautiful cast-
iron bridge to Doggartland House.

The Rye Water and the old ford near
Ryefield House were the inspiration for the
well-known poem 'Comin' thro' the Rye',
usually attributed to Robert Burns,
although known as a traditional song for
many years before him. The poem later

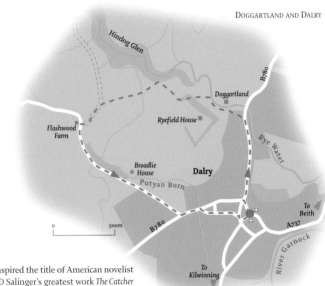

Flashwood Farm · Hindog Glen · Ryefield House · Doggartland · B780 · Rye Water · Broadlie House · Dalry · Putyan Burn · B780 · To Beith · A737 · River Garnock · To Kilwinning

0   500m

inspired the title of American novelist J D Salinger's greatest work *The Catcher in the Rye*.

Follow the waymarked footpath to pass the stables; ignoring any paths branching off – including the new path further up which goes left through a kissing gate and into a young forestry plantation. There are usually muddy sections as the path narrows between a field boundary and the wooded slopes of Hindog Glen.

Corralled between wire fences the path ascends slightly and gets muddier before arriving at the minor road leading to Cunningham Baidland Farm. Just before you join the road look out for an old lime kiln off the side of the path to the right.

Turn left to reach Flashwood Bridge, a small bridge across the road from Flashwood Farm. For a longer walk, you can go right at Flashwood to begin an

ascent of Baidland Hill, home to several wind turbines but also a great viewpoint over much of Ayrshire; otherwise turn left to return to Dalry.

This quiet minor road passes Broadlie House on the left, where in 1892 John Fulton installed one of the first hydroelectric plants in Ayrshire in order to generate electricity for the house. The dam can be seen on the Putyan Burn close to a pedestrian bridge that gave views of the installation to visitors. Continue along the road past a cemetery and into the outskirts of Dalry. The less-minor B780 is reached at a T-junction – turn left and then right at the next fork to return to The Cross.

◄ Clydesdale horse near Dalry

Lynn Glen and Peden's Pulpit

Distance 2km (+2km if starting from Dalry) **Time** 1 hour (+40 mins from Dalry) **Terrain** good earth footpaths and surfaced road; no significant ascent or descent **Map** OS Explorer 333 **Access** trains from Glasgow and Stranraer to Dalry; buses between Glasgow and Ardrossan call at Dalry

The wooded Lynn Glen is a delight, with dramatic waterfalls, a ruined mill and a place in Covenanting history.

This short walk can be started from The Cross in the centre of Dalry. From here, head along Main Street and cross Roche Way into Vennel Street. At the main road, turn right and continue for a distance before branching right into Saltcoats Road. Continue to a small off-road car park just

before the Lynn Bridge on the right.

Carry on along the road to cross the Caaf Water on the Lynn Bridge – it is narrow but does have a pavement. Pass through a small iron gate on the right just after the bridge and proceed along the footpath beyond. After a short distance, ignore a path down to the river on the right where stepping stones once offered a less car-friendly crossing; instead, carry on along the main footpath on the south bank of the Caaf Water into a lush woodland of native birch, hazel and rowan, home to a variety of bird species including wagtails, dippers and the occasional kingfisher.

The walking is pleasant and the route obvious, soon passing a picturesque waterfall known as Lynn Spout where a

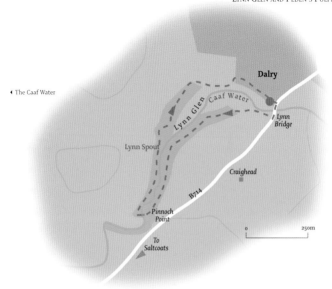

Dalry

Lynn Glen

Caaf Water

Lynn Bridge

Lynn Spout

Craighead

Pinnoch Point

B714

To Saltcoats

◄ The Caaf Water

0   250m

lade and the remains of Craig Mill can be seen. This mill was associated with Kilwinning Abbey, together with Garnock and Sevenacres Mills. Eventually a small wooden footbridge crosses the river to reach Pinnoch Point or 'Peden's Pulpit', named after the famous Covenanting preacher Alexander Peden who was said to have delivered sermons from this large rock overlooking a natural amphitheatre.

In 1682 Peden performed the wedding ceremony of his co-religionists John Brown and Isabel Weir and warned of impending tragedy, telling the bride, 'You have a good man to be your husband, but you will not enjoy him long; prize his company, and keep linen by you to be his winding sheet,

for you will need it when ye are not looking for it, and it will be a bloody one'. Three years later troops commanded by Captain John Graham of Claverhouse shot John Brown for his refusal to take the 1684 Oath of Abjuration and his wife did indeed bury him in the linen sheet she had saved. A memorial to Brown can be visited in the hills above Muirkirk.

Continuing along the footpath, now on the north side of the glen, the walk offers views over Dalry before arriving at the huddle of buildings that make up West Lynn, including West Lynn Villa, the home of artist George Houston RSA, who was born in Dalry in 1869. Follow the surfaced road back to Lynn Bridge and the start.

East Ayrshire is dominated by echoes of its industrial past, driven by the powerful Rivers Irvine and Ayr. The Irvine meanders through Darvel, Newmilns and Galston – former mill towns heavily associated with the weaving industry – before passing the county town of Kilmarnock and entering the Firth of Clyde at Irvine.

The River Ayr has a slightly inauspicious beginning at the former mining village of Glenbuck, home of Bill Shankly and the Glenbuck Cherrypickers football team, the source of a disproportionate number of professional footballers.

Following the river west, Muirkirk forms the start point for a number of excellent walks, including an ascent of the lofty 593m Cairn Table.

The River Ayr Way shadows the river as it accelerates towards the coast, crossing wild moorland and threading its way through wooded glens which shelter picturesque settlements such as Sorn and Failford deep in the historic district of Kyle. Split into three day walks, the whole route makes for an excellent long weekend.

Cairn Table summ

East Ayrshire

The Big Wood at Newmilns

Distance 5km **Time** 1 hour 30
Terrain quiet surfaced roads and woodland
paths; gentle ascent to Woodhead
Map OS Explorer 334 **Access** bus from
Kilmarnock and Stewarton and from
Glasgow and Ayr to Newmilns

**This is a pleasant walk in the woods above
the former lace town of Newmilns.**

Huguenot weavers settled in Newmilns
in the 16th century, establishing a thriving
weaving trade and bringing great
prosperity when the local industry
switched to handlooms in the early 1800s.
The lace mills were a huge employer in the
late 19th century, leading to rapid urban
development before two wars, the Great
Depression and competition from abroad
combined to cause a dramatic decline in
demand. Newmilns gradually changed to
become the commuter town it is now. The
Cross in Castle Street forms the nucleus of
Newmilns' historic buildings, including

The Keep which dates to 1530 and some
impressive townhouses built during this
period of prosperity.

This circular route can be started from
anywhere along the A71 which runs
through town, but if driving it is best to
park in the large lay-by just outside town
on the way to Galston. From the lay-by
the route is indicated by a green Irvine
Valley Paths Network signpost showing
'Newmilns via Woodland'. Follow the
footpath into the woods alongside
Loudoun Gowf Course – the only 'gowf'
course in the world and believed to have
been in use for more than 400 years. Hag
Burn – much prettier than it sounds –
runs along the right-hand side of the path
beyond rowan trees bright with red
berries in late summer. Keep your eyes
peeled for members of a small red
squirrel population that has managed to
survive here. The path continues north
past the grounds of Loudoun Castle – site

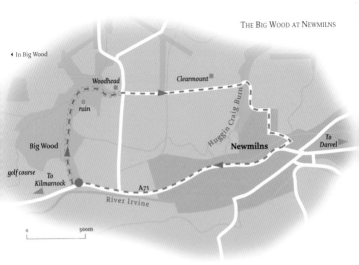

◂ In Big Wood

managed to defeat him in court and the path is now an established right of way.

Continuing onwards, the route curves right and crosses the burn before emerging in a clearing behind Woodhead Farm. Skirt around the buildings to reach a gate to a farm access track. Go through this and the gate opposite to meet a surfaced minor road. Go straight along this quiet road, ignoring Pit Brae which drops down to the A71 on the right and the road leading into the farm on the left. Gaps in the hedgerow provide good views over the Irvine Valley as the road gently descends into the wooded Devil's Basin before winding downhill into Newmilns.

Cross with care at the A71 and turn right to follow the pavement above the river and past the modern housing developments on the outskirts of town back to the walk start at the lay-by.

of the former Loudoun Castle Theme Park. Parts of the castle date back to the 15th century, with major additions made in 1807 before being gutted by fire in 1941. There is rumoured to be a tunnel running to Cessnock Castle more than 2km south beyond the River Irvine.

Further along the footpath, pass a path climbing sharply uphill to the left – ignore this, but look right to see the motte and bailey remains of Arclowdun Castle, once the home of William Wallace's mother Lady Margaret de Lambinus Craufuird. The path you are walking on is known locally as the Lime Road (there are ruined limekilns nearby) and was the subject of 'The Battle of the Lime Road', where from 1878 to 1893 local residents fought Baron Donington of Loudoun Castle for continued access to what was a popular walk. The Baron erected barriers to deter walkers, but residents

25

Darvel and Lanfine Estate

Distance 6.4km Time **2 hours**
Terrain **quiet surfaced roads, earth paths
and good farm tracks; stiff climb to start**
Map **OS Explorer 334** Access **bus from
Kilmarnock and Stewarton and from
Glasgow and Ayr to Darvel**

**A varied circuit offering good views over
Darvel and the Irvine Valley before
returning via the exotically-planted
Lanfine Estate – watch out for the family
of 'wild boars' too.**

Head south from Darvel's Main Street
along Ranoldcoup Road to reach the Grade
B-listed stone bridge across the River
Irvine. There is a public car park just after
leaving the main road.

Cross the bridge to accompany the road
as it winds uphill under a canopy of
deciduous trees. You'll encounter a series
of switchbacks on the journey towards
Dyke Farm, each furnished with a bench

and increasingly pleasing views across the
valley and Darvel. The climb is rewarded by
a final view over the Irvine Valley as you
reach a kissing gate just before Dyke Farm.

Go through the gate and follow the
narrow grassy path corralled between post-
and-wire fences, bearing eastwards. When
you come to a wider tree-lined corridor,
climb uphill – after rain this could be
muddy, but any inconvenience is short-
lived. At the edge of woodland, a kissing
gate gives access to a small picnic area.

Turn right to enter the mixed
woodland and follow a pleasant narrow
path crossing wooden duckboards and
footbridges where indicated by waymarkers
and staying alert for sightings of squirrels
and deer in this wonderfully wild section
of the route.

Upon reaching a wide forest ride, turn
right to meet a farm track and right again
before following the surfaced road past

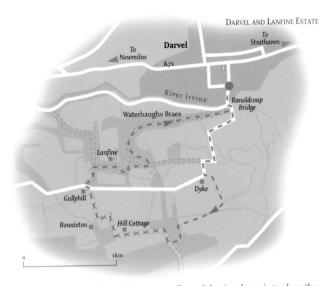

Hill Cottage. This access road turns right, then left and right again as it drops downhill to rejoin the minor road about 1km west of Dyke Farm. Turn left and then immediately right to enter Lanfine Estate.

Lanfine was inherited by Thomas Brown, a medical doctor and professor of botany at Glasgow University, in the 1820s, and he planted many exotic trees and shrubs as well as vast tracts of mixed woodland. Brown also amassed one of the greatest collections of minerals and fossils in Scotland, and his collections can be seen at Edinburgh and Glasgow Universities.

Follow the surfaced estate road and turn right where indicated by a black signpost for Darvel. After another 200m, take the right fork at a path junction, again towards Darvel. The walking is easy along these well-made tracks, but keep an eye out for a

smaller path leaving the main track on the left – the now-familiar signpost is again present, but confusingly shows two options for the return to Darvel. The small path has been laid with aggregate and shadows a small burn downhill through the trees before arriving at a roadbridge on the main estate access road. Turn right along this.

A tall mesh fence running alongside the road contains a family of pigs – very close to wild boar in appearance – which have been introduced to 27 acres of woodland in an attempt to promote natural regeneration of the woodland and supplement the estate farm business. Amble along the estate road (watching for any foraging pigs within the enclosure) to reach the gatehouse by the Ranoldcoup Road Bridge and return to Darvel.

◀ Rhododendron in Lanfine Estate

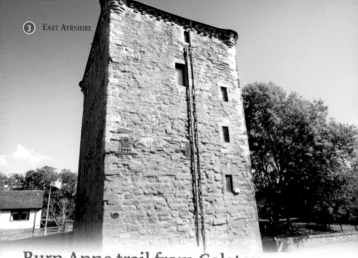

Burn Anne trail from Galston

Distance 8.7km **Time** 3 hours
Terrain good earth and grass footpaths
and surfaced road; gently undulating
Map OS Explorer 334 **Access** bus from
Kilmarnock and Stewarton and from
Glasgow and Ayr to Galston

**An easy circuit of the woods and meadows
of the Irvine Valley.**

This pleasant circuit begins from the
public car park opposite the stronghold of
Barr Castle – formerly known as Lockhart's
Tower – in the town of Galston. The whole
Irvine Valley has historic links to William
Wallace, and Barr Castle was reputed to
have housed Wallace and his men as they
evaded English troops. Wallace invented a
kind of handball game played against the
castle walls in order to keep his men fit,
and this unique game was played in the
area until the 1930s.

Leave the car park and turn right to reach
a bridge over the Burn Anne, then turn left
onto Cemetery Road. Follow this quiet
road through a residential area and past
the cemetery before crossing back over the
burn and bearing left to reach the B7037
towards Sorn. Cross this and turn right
along the pavement as directed by the
obvious blue signs. Before reaching the
small bridge, go through a wooden kissing
gate on the left to enter Burnhouse Brae
Wood. The earth path beyond is initially
corralled between fences before opening
out in the cool woodland and beginning to
climb high above the Burn Anne.

With occasional glimpses of Irvine Valley
farmland, the path generally remains in
the trees before switchbacking down to a
minor road. Turn right to cross the burn
again and take the path on the left after the
bridge. This trail continues through the

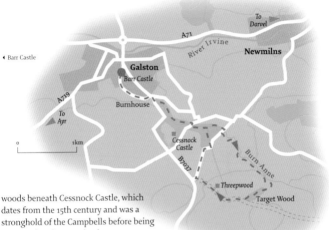

◄ Barr Castle

woods beneath Cessnock Castle, which dates from the 15th century and was a stronghold of the Campbells before being converted to the mansion house seen today. Keep right at a fork before descending to the burn at a wooden footbridge. Cross this and turn right on the far side. The trail eventually reaches a surfaced minor road via a gate – pass through this and turn right along the road for a short distance. On the left, just after a passing place, is an obvious blue arrow and carved wooden sign indicating the continuation of the route. Go through the kissing gate and onto the narrow often overgrown path. This meanders through a series of meadows, sometimes close to the burn and at others high above at the field boundary. At any junctions you can take either fork as the paths always converge.

On this section of the walk keep an eye out for deer and fox and plenty of birdlife, including ravens and hawks. Interpretation boards offer flora and fauna identification guides further on. At an obvious path junction by some carved wooden signs, go left to carry on along the main path which follows the course of the burn. Eventually, it leaves the water and curves uphill (right) to Target Wood, but not before offering panoramic views across the county to Arran beyond.

Follow the path through the open woodland to reach a minor road. Turn right and continue to enjoy the views as this drops downhill towards Threepwood Farm. Carry on through the farm on this quiet road to meet another road bearing right just before Sornhill and marked with a blue signpost. This takes you towards the woodland encountered on the outward route – enter the trees through a kissing gate. The path beyond threads its way through the trees to emerge by the wooden footbridge over the burn. From here, retrace your steps to Barr Castle.

Loudoun Hill from Darvel

Distance 11.5km **Time** 3 hours
Terrain grass and earth footpaths and
surfaced road; the section on the railway
path can be overgrown; no significant
ascent until the final summit climb
Map OS Landranger 71 **Access** bus from
Kilmarnock and Stewarton and from
Glasgow and Ayr to Darvel

An easy level walk along an abandoned
railway line, followed by an ascent of the
landmark Loudoun Hill, gateway to the
Irvine Valley.

Sir Alexander Fleming, the discoverer of
penicillin, was born at Lochfield Farm near
Darvel in 1881 and a bust in his honour sits
in Hastings Square along with the curious-
looking 'Dagon Stone'. Begin the walk
from the square and head along Main
Street until you reach Cemetery Road on
the outskirts of the town. Take this road
left uphill and through the remains of a
railway bridge before a footpath is
apparent on the right. Follow this path
alongside and then up onto the old railway
line, bearing eastwards. The going is level
and quite easy, though potentially
overgrown for the first section. The
undergrowth soon eases as Darvel is left
behind, and walkers are rewarded with
open views of farm and moorland.

Route finding is not difficult – simply
follow the line of the railway. However,
there is a short diversion where the path
heads sharply left up a small flight of steps
and is corralled between two fences. Follow
the obvious path and waymarkers as
appropriate and follow the guidance of

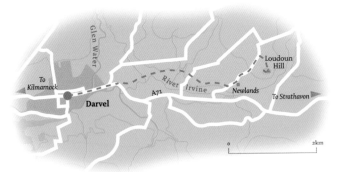

local farmers and rangers who often introduce temporary diversions. The railway drops down into several cuttings to pass beneath bridges, and the path narrows to remain on the high ground. In reality, it is often easier to follow the route of the railway to go under the bridge as well, but do not cross any fences apart from at stiles and gates.

Continue along the grassy path through an area dotted with iron slag, the byproduct of iron smelting. Eventually the path rises before ending abruptly at the top of a ruined bridge support, with further supports crossing farmland ahead. Descend as directed to cross a wall and turn right along a lane to reach a minor road above the A71. Turn left and begin a steep road climb towards the hill. The road begins to circle around the west of the hill before you come to a gate on the right – go through this to follow a footpath across farmland via a series of white waymarks. When the final boundary fence is crossed, turn right to contour around the base of

the hill before following the well-worn grassy path up to the top.

Close to the summit is a plaque which commemorates the battle fought in the area in 1307 between Robert the Bruce and an English force led by Aymer de Valance, one of three military encounters associated with Loudoun Hill. Eleven years earlier, during the Wars of Scottish Independence, William Wallace is also thought to have got into a fight nearby and there is a modern sculpture marking his victory close to the car park to the east of the hill. Further to the east is the site of the Battle of Drumclog, in which a small group of Covenanters defeated an army led by John Graham of Claverhouse in 1679.

The steep pull up to the rocky 316m summit is rewarded by panoramic views over Ayrshire, Lanarkshire, the Firth of Clyde and Arran. The south face of Loudoun Hill provides several routes for rock climbers, but it is advisable to return via the ascent route and retrace your steps back to Darvel.

◀ Loudoun Hill summit

Muirkirk railway loop

Distance 3.5km **Time** 1hour 30
Terrain good footpaths and surfaced
minor road; no significant ascent
Map OS Landranger 71 **Access** buses from
Glasgow and Ayr stop at Muirkirk, 1km
from Kames

**A straightforward circuit of the moorland
south of Muirkirk, following the course
of a long-abandoned railway and canal.**

From the car park at Kames, turn away
from the information board and hills on
the horizon ahead to take the path on the
right adjacent to the car park entrance.
Go through the gate and onto a well-made
footpath, following the route of a former
railway which has been refurbished to
become part of the River Ayr Way. This
long-distance path is well waymarked with
red double-headed arrows where necessary.

The railway opened in 1848, designed to
transport minerals from the local pits to
the ironwork furnaces in Auchinleck. Now
long gone, the railway bed makes a
convenient footpath.

Carry on along this until you come to a
River Ayr Way marker post, where you drop
down onto the bank of a former canal –
dug much earlier than the railway in 1790
to transport coal by barge from the
Lightshaw, Auldhouseburn and Crossflat
pits. At a pair of kissing gates turn left as
indicated by the waymarkers and continue
along a path corralled neatly between two
fences. After a short distance the path
reaches a quiet country road by a kissing
gate – go through the gate and turn right
to leave the River Ayr Way.

The lane heads uphill through the
remains of an old railway bridge to reach

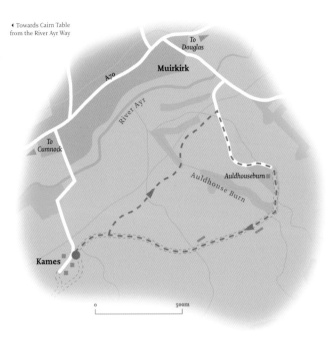

◀ Towards Cairn Table
from the River Ayr Way

Auldhouseburn House, dating back to 1610 though modified in 1884. There is rumoured to be an escape tunnel running from the house to a nearby burn – a reminder of the house's historical links with the Covenanters. Keep left at the entrance drive to skirt around the house and outbuildings, then trend right to go past a large poultry unit and through a gate into open farmland.

Now on a good farm track, there are panoramic views over the moorland and hills south of Muirkirk, including popular Cairn Table with its summit war memorial. Later the prominent clocktower of Kames Institute dominates the view – built as a recreation centre for the miners formerly housed in the village, but now sadly neglected. The path continues through a series of gates before rejoining the outward path to return to the car park.

Twa Brigs and the drove road

Distance **5.4km** Time **2 hours**
Terrain **good footpaths, surfaced minor
road and a section of the first tarmacadam
road experiment; gently undulating**
Map **OS Landranger 71** Access **buses from
Glasgow and Ayr stop at Muirkirk, 1km
from Kames**

**This is a varied circular walk which visits
two historic bridges in the moorland
south of Muirkirk.**

From the car park at Kames, simply head
towards the information board next to the
wooden shelter and bear right along the
waymarked River Ayr Way. There has been
some confusion with waymarker arrow
colours in this area, so be careful not to
head across the moorland towards Cairn
Table by accident. The correct path passes
behind the Kames Institute and adjacent

houses, before reaching a minor road
running alongside the motorsport circuit
and golf course. Turn left along this road
and continue southwest to a large
information board stating that the track
underfoot is, in fact, the product of local
man John Loudon McAdam's early
experiments with road surfacing and the
ruins behind the board formed McAdam's
residence in the late 1700s. McAdam moved
to the property to manage the 9th Earl of
Dundonald's tar works before buying the
company himself in 1790.

A short distance from the ruin, the
earthworks associated with the facility are
visible – turn right where indicated to

descend alongside the outline of a row of miners' cottages to reach Tibbie's Brig (originally Garpel Bridge). Tibbie (Isobel) Pagan, a poet and contemporary of Robert Burns, lived in a small cottage beside the bridge which doubled as a lively drinking den. Born with a deformed foot, a squint and a large tumour on her side, Tibbie was also an excellent singer and is thought by some to be the originator of a poem made famous by Burns, 'Ca' the Yowes tae the Knowes'. From here go down to the river on the east of the bridge and follow the narrow riverside footpath.

Cross a couple of simple footbridges before striking out into the rolling countryside. The narrow but obvious path takes a pleasant meandering route over the varied terrain by the scenic Garpel Water before a series of eroded waymarker posts indicate a sharp left turn across the moorland. Take care to follow these to reach a well-made drove road. This ancient track linking Muirkirk with Sanquhar some 28km away was much used by coach traffic in the late 1700s as part of a route from Glasgow to Dumfries.

Turn right and proceed along this to reach the second bridge across the Garpel Water – Sanquhar Brig. Formerly of wooden construction, a modern metal footbridge provides access to the moorland and hills beyond. Spend some time exploring the various wells in the area, including Minister's Well, as well as the nearby Bronze Age remains. The return is along the drove road, ignoring your outward path branching left, to reach a cairn commemorating McAdam, built from stone taken from the remains of his kilns. Continue along the path for 150m to rejoin the outward route, but this time pass the front of the Kames Institute to reach the car park.

◄ Tibbie's Brig

35

Cairn Table

Distance 8.8km **Time** 3 hours
Terrain grass/earth footpaths and good
aggregate tracks; very boggy; relentless
ascent to summit **Map** OS Landranger 71
Access buses from Glasgow and Ayr stop
at Muirkirk, 1km from Kames

A circular hillwalk to the summit of
a popular Ayrshire landmark which
returns via the old Muirkirk to Sanquhar
drove road.

The walk is relatively straightforward,
with good paths all the way but a high
chance of encountering some pretty boggy
patches. Choose your footwear accordingly
– it is not unusual to encounter welly-clad
walkers on this route!

Begin from the car park adjacent to the
Kames Institute – an information board
shows the route, but the colours used on
the map may not necessarily match those
shown on the route waymarkers. Continue

past the board and ignore the paths
forking right to begin a short ascent to a
gate with adjacent stile. Crossing the stile
takes you out into an expanse of farmland
dotted with relics of the area's industrial
past. Evidence of lead, coal and iron ore
mining can be seen, along with traces of an
aggregate path beneath the grass.

The path quickly degenerates as it
winds over and around the many springs
emerging from the northwest slopes of
Cairn Table. Water from one of these
springs – Cairntable Cauldron – is
rumoured to have been in demand by
the Picts to create a heather-based
homebrew. A series of wooden
duckboards and bridges have been
installed to ease progress over the worst
of the bog, but once through a kissing
gate and onto the moorland proper the
going gets quite tricky after rain.

Follow the path alongside a fence and

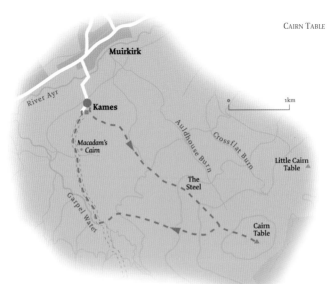

Muirkirk

River Ayr

Kames

Macadam's Cairn

Auldhouse Burn

Crossflat Burn

Little Cairn Table

The Steel

Garpel Water

Cairn Table

1km

drystane dyke, known locally as the March Fence – the gradient begins to steepen and the path becomes rocky as the spur named The Steel is gained. From this 413m spot height, it is a short, sharp climb to reach a path junction below the Cairn Table summit – either turn left to take the gradual track or carry straight on to cross a small bridge and ascend a narrower, rough footpath. Regardless of route, you soon gain the rocky 593m summit, where a huge cairn, triangulation pillar and direction indicator jostle for position.

The cairn was built in 1920 in memory of local men and women who served in the Great War. Further east are the remains of two prehistoric cairns, one of which has been severely depleted to provide building material for the memorial and is now topped by the trig pillar, and one

beyond which is relatively undisturbed. The views from the summit are extensive, with the Isle of Arran often visible on the western horizon and Ben Lomond to the north.

Return to the path junction and take the left fork to descend roughly west across grouse moorland. In August the purple heather bloom is particularly stunning, and a haven for birds such as hen harrier, curlew and lapwing. This narrower path is rougher and less eroded than the ascent route, but nonetheless easy going, with ample opportunity to enjoy the views over the Garpel Water before descending to the old drove road to Sanquhar. Turn right to follow the path back into Kames, passing a cairn to John Loudon McAdam and the ruins of his old house at Springhill.

◀ On the way to Cairn Table

River Ayr Way: Glenbuck to Sorn

Distance 27.8km Time 8 hours
Terrain footpaths and surfaced roads;
gently undulating Map OS Landranger 71
Access no public transport to Glenbuck,
but buses from Cumnock and Kilmarnock
stop at Muirkirk and Sorn

Follow the infant River Ayr through wild
moorland rich in natural and industrial
history to the attractive village of Sorn.

The mining village of Glenbuck was
founded in 1650, but lacked a regular
source of employment until a successful
ironworks was established in 1790 and
caused the population to rise. The village
remained in existence until the 1930s when
the last residents were rehoused in nearby
Muirkirk and opencast mining claimed the
remaining buildings.

Glenbuck's claim to fame, however, is
the astonishing number of professional
footballers it produced – over fifty –
among them the great Bill Shankly who

was capped by Scotland 12 times and
went on to become a legendary manager
of Liverpool Football Club. There is a
memorial plaque celebrating Shankly's
achievements at the start of the walk.

The walk begins at a hide on the north
side of the loch. Head west to reach the
large River Ayr sculpture consisting of a
huge slab made of cast sand from Ayr
Beach. The equivalent slab at Ayr is
constructed from cast coal dust from the
opencast mine at Glenbuck, and the two
sculptures are aligned with each other.
Continue along the road as indicated by
waymarker posts to reach the Bill Shankly
memorial, and turn left to follow the road
south for a short distance. Leave the road
to follow a footpath running parallel to it
but behind a fence and hedge – this avoids
the junction with the A70 and leads to a
crossing a short distance to the west.

Now on the south side of the road the
route follows the course of the Caledonian

Glenbuck Loch

Wedder
Hill

Middlefield
Law

Greenock Water

Glenbuck
Loch

To
Douglas

A70

A70

Sorn

B743

Muirkirk

A70

Little
Cairn Table

Airds Moss

River Ayr

A70

Garpel Water

Cairn Table

0   4km

Wardlaw Hill

Railway line across the moors, passing the wooden remains of the former Glenbuck Station platform on the right. The railway track bed makes for easy walking and gives views towards the hills on the border with Lanarkshire. The route passes numerous ruins and industrial relics, with the huge opencast mine on the other side of the road a reminder that Ayrshire is still a major supplier of coal to Scotland and beyond. The route briefly detours from the railway line at Crossflat, heading right for a short distance before leaving the minor road by a stile on the left and passing through farmland to rejoin the railway path just before Kames.

The car park at Kames is the starting point for walkers heading up Cairn Table. Stay on the path indicated which goes around the back of the Kames Institute, built in 1904 as a community resource for the hundreds of families once housed in miners' rows nearby. Returning to a roughly-finished track the route continues southwest away from the river to a large information board stating that the track underfoot is the product of local man John

Loudon McAdam's early experiments with road surfacing and the ruins behind the board are what's left of McAdam's residence in the late 1700s. McAdam moved to the property to manage the 9th Earl of Dundonald's tar works before buying the company himself in 1790. A short distance from the ruin the earthworks associated with the facility are visible – turn right where indicated to descend alongside the outline of a row of miners' cottages to reach Tibbie's Brig (originally Garpel Bridge). Tibbie Pagan, a poet and contemporary of Robert Burns, ran a small inn adjacent to the bridge.

Cross the bridge and bear right on the path, joining a rough track for a short distance and then turning left up steps to reach another dismantled railway. Follow this west until, after 1km, there is a right turn towards Upper Wellwood – take this, turning left onto a footpath before you reach the buildings. The path leads through the woods, passing an information board for the fenced martyr's grave close to the burn below, before rejoining the river for a pleasant meander to Wellwood Bridge. Remain on the south side of the river, passing through a small patch of woodland and crossing the A70 where indicated next to an electricity substation at Nether Wellwood.

Another short section of woodland follows; you then cross the river at the roadbridge and enter the field on the far side. Continue along the well-maintained path before crossing back over at a footbridge above a set of stepping stones (these can be used if the river is low enough). The route is now entering the enormous bog known as Airds Moss – protected by the RSPB as a valuable habitat for hen harriers, peregrine falcons, merlins and grouse. Pass a memorial to John Lapraik, an 18th-century poet who farmed in the area. The path later passes the remains of a very early ironworks, the lade and reservoir still visible between the path and river. Cross another footbridge to reach the B743 at Greenock Mains. Turn left, cross the old sandstone Greenock Bridge and almost immediately descend steps to rejoin the riverside path by the Greenock Water, a tributary of the Ayr.

After a short distance cross the mouth of the Whitehaugh Water via a footbridge and pass the precarious suspension bridge known locally as Fisherman's Bridge. Thankfully there is no need to cross it to continue the route. The path heads away from the road once more and meanders roughly parallel to the river, before climbing steeply onto higher ground above the plantations surrounding Upper Heilar. The path bypasses steep cliffs to head across moorland and along field boundaries before dropping down to Merkland Burn and then climbing onto the wooden duckboards encircling steep Castle Hill. At the end of the walkway the path crosses the aptly-named Wyndy Burn as it joins the river and continues alongside farmland to the west end of Hole Holm. Here, a path leads away from the river into woodland to pass a steep cliff – the drop from the path is near-vertical at one point, though well protected.

Back at the riverside the path traverses the wooded slopes of Haggis Bank, passes a flooded limestone quarry in the trees and two ruinous limekilns, and continues into the Dalgainbank Plantation. Ignore any paths leading down towards the river and carry on along the obvious path to reach the B743 east of Sorn. Turn left and enter the village along the Main Street – you'll find a general store and post office here, as well as the Sorn Inn located in an 18th-century building at the west end of the village.

River Ayr Way: Sorn to Stair

Distance 18.8km **Time** 7 hours
Terrain well-made aggregate footpaths
and surfaced roads; gently undulating
Map OS Landranger 70 **Access** bus stops
at Sorn, but there is no public transport
to Stair

**From humble beginnings the River Ayr
is now a wide, powerful waterway,
coursing through rocky gorges and
elegant estate policies.**

From the Sorn Inn, walk west and cross
the 18th-century Old Bridge. Turn right on
the far side and climb along the quiet road
to gain views across the fields and river to
Sorn Castle. A footpath leaves the road
through a kissing gate on the right,
skirting the field boundary before
dropping into woodland beside the river.

Continue along the wooded slopes by a
good path on the south side of the water.
Eventually dropping slightly to follow the
river closely, the path skirts Daldorch
House before Catrine comes into view.
Cross the river at a footbridge, bear left and
enter Catrine Voes Local Nature Reserve.

The Voes (reservoirs) were once used to
store water prior to being released to drive
a large mill wheel, and now form a habitat
for a variety of wildlife. A path through
the Voes emerges at a road junction – head
in either direction to descend to Laigh
Road and, keeping left, reach the main
road through Catrine. Turn right along
St Germain Street to reach Mill Square,
then left along Bridge Street to cross the
river at Timmer Bridge in front of the
A M Brown Institute.

Turn right and cross Bogend Burn by a
footbridge to reach a surfaced minor road
running past a row of bungalows. Remain
on the road until it curves left towards the
sewage works, where a footpath continues
straight ahead to follow the river. A good
path runs through woods before climbing
steps and continuing along the clifftop.

The path slopes down a wooded valley
before passing beneath the A76 at Howford
Bridge. Ignore the left-hand path for
Catrine House and instead drop down to
cross the Old Howford Bridge, in use for
200 years until the 1950s. Continue along

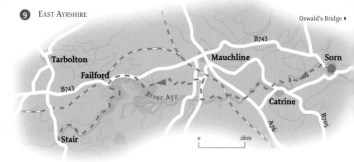

the former main road, passing a pair of sandstone abutments that once supported a footbridge in the policies of the former Ballochmyle Estate. Cross a stile on the left a short way on and bear left to enter the woodland beneath the road. Just after a footbridge is a vertical cliff face bearing prehistoric cup and ring markings alongside more recent 18th-century 'grafitti'.

The path wanders through the wooded valley high above the river, passing beneath the immense Ballochmyle Railway Viaduct which incorporates the longest masonry railway arch ever built at 55.17m. From the viaduct follow the path until it emerges from the woods and leads through farmland to meet a minor road at Haugh Farm. Turn right to take the Mauchline road north to Haughyett Farm, going left here along the minor road to Barskimming Road, where another left turn will take you to a footpath just past Woodlands Farm on the right. This runs across farmland, tightly corralled between two fences as it skirts around the private Barskimming Estate policies. The route runs by a group of trees around a flooded quarry, source of much of the sandstone used to construct the buildings of

Glasgow. After passing through a dark plantation and further farmland, the footpath eventually reaches the B743 outside the small village of Failford. Turn left and follow the road into the village with care. It consists of little more than a row of almshouses, one of them housing the Failford Inn.

Leave the road via a footpath at the west end of the village and drop down into an attractive gorge, crossing a small burn and climbing a flight of steps. The easy-going path leads left with obvious waymarking as the river glides over vast sandstone slabs below. It returns to the riverside for a while, before another flight of steps leads up to the boundary of the Ayr Gorge Woodlands Reserve. Follow the field margins downhill to the river, now in more open countryside, before re-entering woods at Wellflat Bank. The fortified Stair House is visible on the other side of the river, and beyond that Stair Parish Church.

Follow the path past a former sluice gate and lade to reach the road at the small settlement of Milton adjacent to the Stair Bridge Toll Cottage. To reach Stair itself, turn left and follow the road with care over the narrow bridge and down into the village.

River Ayr Way: Stair to Ayr

Distance 20km **Time** 7 hours
Terrain well-made aggregate footpaths
and surfaced roads; gently undulating
Map OS Landranger 70 **Access** no public
transport to Stair, but Ayr is served by
numerous bus routes and a train station.

This final section of the River Ayr Way
follows the river through open farmland
and estate policies before entering the
historic county town of Ayr and reaching
journey's end at Ayr Harbour.

Head away from Stair Bridge into the
tiny settlement of Milton, passing the Stair
Bridge Toll Cottage on the right, and
follow the B730 to a small lay-by on the left
as the road swings right. Take the path
through fields to return to the riverside
600m downstream of the bridge. Directly
across the water is the old whetstone mine
at Dalmore. The path shadows the river for
some distance on the floodplain beneath
the impressive Enterkine House on Holm
Bank to the north.

Pass under the Enterkine Viaduct, erected
in 1872 to carry the Ayr to Cumnock
Railway but now utilised by coal wagons
from the various opencast mines nearby.
Carry on to Gadgirth Bridge, staying on the
north side of the river to enter the
woodland east of Annbank. There are
several small paths to the village, but
ignore these to reach a small picnic area.
Follow Dunlop Avenue to the main road
and turn left along Braeside to Mill Road,
which is a left turn bearing southeast. The
track continues left past an old nursery to
reach Privick Mill. A path on the right
skirts around the mill buildings and
rejoins the river atop a steep bank.

On the opposite bank are the remains of
the Old Ha', a castle on a rocky outcrop
projecting out into the river. Beneath this,
the river is forced between rocks, creating a
16m-deep pool known as Auld Ha' Weel.

Cross Tarholm Bridge further on and
briefly follow the B744 as it curves right,
leaving it as it bends left to enter a section

43

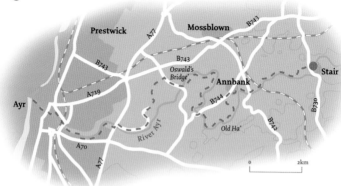

of pleasant woodland. A good path above the river enters a deep wooded gorge, formerly part of the Auchincruive Estate, and rises to Wallace's Seat, a viewpoint where William Wallace was reputed to have hidden from English forces in the 13th century. Descend to the riverside again and head through Craighall Wood, the path following the river on a a wide arc around Pheasant Nook before leaving the water to dive through the trees. At a path junction keep right to continue along the riverside, before leaving the woods and entering a field known as Three Green Knights Park after the three grassy mounds in the field. The path takes you to the road adjacent to the 1826 Oswald's Bridge.

Cross the bridge and pass the entrance to Auchincruive House, taking a signed cyclepath immediately after a couple of college buildings on the opposite side of the road. The track passes woods and grazing land before joining a surfaced road by a number of smallholdings. Follow this road – punishing for the footsore –

towards the busy A77. Turn sharp right and pass the Scottish SPCA centre to reach a cyclepath adjacent to the road. Turn left, cross the roadbridge and then follow steps down to the river close to a series of stepping stones at Overmills, the site of a mill since the 13th century. Closed in 1960, it was the last working grain mill on the River Ayr and was demolished in 1963.

Now head under the road onto the River Ayr Walk past pleasant fields and Kyle Academy rugby pitch. Cross a footbridge to pass an 18th-century limekiln with a plaque commemorating the creation of the River Ayr Walk in 1910. The path comes close to the A70, but remains within the trees before descending a flight of steps to reach Craigholm Bridge. Cross this, over a large pool in the river known as Craigie Weel, and turn left on the far side. The riverside path runs through the grounds of Craigie Estate, which is now part of the University of the West of Scotland.

Pass Ayr College and a series of weirs in the river originally supplying the Nether

Burns statue in Ayr ▶

Mill of Ayr, an ancient mill dating to 1531, which was demolished in 1941. Continue beneath the Victoria Bridge carrying the A79, pass the fire station on the right and head under the Water Bridge carrying the railway line between Glasgow and Stranraer. The path continues past Turner's Bridge, erected by A M Turner to permit workers to cross to his brewery which once stood on the south side of the river. Just before reaching the Auld Bridge, bear right to pass the Black Bull Hotel, then left to cross the bridge. On the south side, head up Auld Bridge Street to High Street, turn right and cross New Bridge Street to enter Boat Vennel. This lane houses Loudoun Hall, Ayr's oldest house erected in 1513.

Leaving Boat Vennel continue along South Harbour Street – cylindrical pillars in the river behind the Waterside Restaurant are the remains of a steel railway bridge erected in 1899 and demolished in 1978. The turret atop a sloping wall on the left is known as Miller's Folly, built by an eccentric Victorian called John Miller who purchased the former Cromwell barracks in 1870 and claimed to be a Baron as a result of owning the citadel. Erected in 1652 the citadel was one of five forts established by the Protectorate of Scotland and once housed 1200 Cromwellian soldiers. Pass the Citadel Leisure Centre and a selection of modern flats to reach the quayside south of Ayr Harbour. Upon reaching a former shipyard slip, now housing the fishing boat *Watchful*, turn right and cross a footbridge at the end of the slip. This provides access to the South Pier guarding the mouth of the harbour and extending into the bay.

The lighthouse at the end of the pier marks the western extremity of the River Ayr, and thus the terminus of the River Ayr Way. If the weather is good, the Heads of Ayr are visible at the southern end of the sandy bay and the distinctive mountainous profile of Arran dominates the horizon.

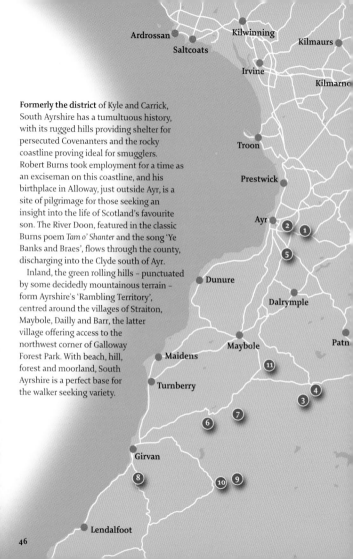

Formerly the district of Kyle and Carrick, South Ayrshire has a tumultuous history, with its rugged hills providing shelter for persecuted Covenanters and the rocky coastline proving ideal for smugglers. Robert Burns took employment for a time as an exciseman on this coastline, and his birthplace in Alloway, just outside Ayr, is a site of pilgrimage for those seeking an insight into the life of Scotland's favourite son. The River Doon, featured in the classic Burns poem *Tam o' Shanter* and the song 'Ye Banks and Braes', flows through the county, discharging into the Clyde south of Ayr.

Inland, the green rolling hills – punctuated by some decidedly mountainous terrain – form Ayrshire's 'Rambling Territory', centred around the villages of Straiton, Maybole, Dailly and Barr, the latter village offering access to the northwest corner of Galloway Forest Park. With beach, hill, forest and moorland, South Ayrshire is a perfect base for the walker seeking variety.

South Ayrshire

Oswald's Bridge and Auchincruive

Distance 5.5km **Time** 1 hour 30
Terrain earth footpaths, gently undulating
woodland tracks and quiet minor road
Map OS Landranger 70 **Access** bus
between Mauchline and Ayr stops at the
estate gates

One of the longer routes on the
Auchincruive Estate, this walk combines
a stretch of pleasant riverside with
woodland trails and a return through the
estate arboretum.

Leaving the Oswald's Bridge car park,
turn right to reach the estate entrance just
before the bridge. Enter and follow the
riverbank to pick up blue waymarker
arrows and descend a gravel slope to the
riverside promenade. This is the beginning
of Auchincruive's famous Hanging
Gardens, built in the 1830s as a work
creation scheme for unemployed miners.
The terraced sandstone walls that

comprise the gardens include semi-circular
pier structures at regular intervals and one
section is buttressed; depending on the
season the narrow planted terraces can be
a riot of cascading colour. The first section
of easy walking accompanies the River Ayr
– watch for heron hunting in the slow-
moving flow as you head upstream.

Continue through a wooden kissing
gate, with the trees of Brockle Wood now
forming a canopy overhead. The path
narrows and becomes softer underfoot to
reach a raised opening in a sturdy stone
wall. Go up and over the well-worn steps to
carry on along the path. The ancient
hamlet of Millholm was situated nearby,
and part of the riverbank was washed away
in 1966 to reveal an old mill lade.

Ignore a path branching left uphill to
carry on along the root-strewn path rising
above the river. Shortly after it has made a
180-degree meander, turn left and away

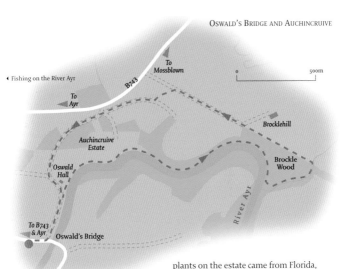

◄ Fishing on the River Ayr

from the riverbank to move deeper into the woods. Pass a flight of wooden steps to the right to continue along the main path. There are numerous smaller trails leading through the woods, but the blue arrows make navigation easy. A small burn accompanies the route as it winds through the trees, assisted where necessary by steps, before emerging onto a farm track. Turn left to follow the woodland boundary to a surfaced minor road by Brocklehill Farm.

Follow the road left and downhill through farmland with unrestricted pastoral views. Watch for a gate on the left at a small lay-by, going through this as indicated by the blue waymarker arrow to re-enter the estate grounds. Take the middle grassy track heading diagonally left to enter the arboretum, home to a vast variety of trees. Many of the trees and plants on the estate came from Florida, Jamaica, Bengal and China (regions in which 18th-century owner Richard Oswald had financial interests) and the ornamental gardens were laid out in the style of Capability Brown. Auchincruive was one of the first estates to have hothouses – in which were grown such delicacies as grapes, figs and pineapples. Sugar seedlings were also grown and exported to Oswald's Florida plantation.

Follow the post-and-wire fence to reach the Nellie's Gate estate entrance – continue straight ahead onto a surfaced estate road which skirts a sports field to reach Oswald Hall. Built in 1767, Robert Adam designed the interior and the majority of the external façade, as well as Oswald's Temple, a castellated temple or teahouse which stands nearby. Follow the road above the river back down to Oswald's Bridge and the car park at the start.

49

Three Green Knights Trail

Distance 3.5km **Time** 1 hour **Terrain** earth
footpaths and woodland tracks; one
gentle climb **Map** OS Landranger 70
Access bus between Mauchline and Ayr
stops at the estate gates

**A short, gentle walk along the south bank
of the River Ayr and through the mixed
woodland of the Auchincruive Estate.**

Leaving the Oswald's Bridge car park,
turn right to reach the bridge, erected in
1826 and named after Richard Oswald,
the 18th-century tobacco merchant and
slave trader who built the classical
Auchincruive House in 1767. Immediately
after crossing the bridge, turn left as
indicated by a green waymarker to drop
down onto a small footpath winding
along the south bank of the River Ayr,

which is wide and sluggish this close to
the sea.

As you skirt along the river, look out for
herons and dippers feeding; there are
numerous little bays that make ideal spots
for contemplation or a cup of tea.
Supported by wooden railings and steps
across the worst of the obstacles, the path
reaches a stile just before a small wooden
shack. Cross this into a field, turning left to
follow its grassy boundary, before crossing
another stile to access an area of mixed
deciduous and coniferous woodland,
which consists mainly of beech, oak, Scots
pine and Japanese larch.

The easy path climbs gently to the top
corner of the Three Knights Field, named
after the three mounds visible in the field.
The views over Oswald Hall, renamed from

◄ Pathway by River Ayr

Auchincruive House in 1927 when the estate was sold by the Oswald family and became the West of Scotland College of Agriculture, are splendid. The estate became the Scottish Agricultural College in 1990, but plans to redevelop the site were approved in 2011. Looking over the river, the panorama encompasses the Hanging Gardens, Mount Charles Wood and the Carrick Hills, extending to Arran on a clear day.

Don't cross the stile that you'll see here; instead turn left as indicated by the green waymarker arrow and continue along the easy forest path high above the river. Re-emerging from the forest canopy, turn sharp right to plunge back onto a wooded track which forms a section of the River Ayr Way. Though mostly firm underfoot, there can be a few muddy patches criss-crossed by mountain bike tyre marks. Go through the gate at the end of the woodland and onto a grass farm track which leads to a gate by the road a short distance southeast of Oswald's Bridge. Turn right along the road to return to the car park.

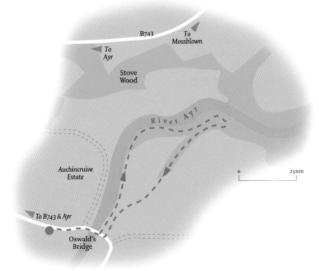

Bennan Hill and the monument

Distance 8.45km Time 3 hours
Terrain grass and earth footpaths and
surfaced road; two steep climbs
Map OS Landranger 77 Access bus from
Ayr to Straiton

A pleasant circuit over the hills
overlooking one of Scotland's favourite
villages located in what is known as
Ayrshire's 'Rambling Territory'.

In common with most of the waymarked
walks in Ayrshire, there is an information
board in the car park in Straiton indicating
a selection of walks in the area. This walk
must surely be the finest, offering
panoramic views over the village and
surrounding countryside. From the car
park return to the road and turn right,
crossing the burn on a separate wooden
footbridge to pass 16th-century St
Cuthbert's Church with colourful
stained-glass windows and a crow-
stepped gable. Enter the village and
continue along the pavement, passing
McCandlish Hall and The Black Bull
Hotel. Straiton was created by

Thomas Kennedy, Earl of Cassilis as a
model village in the mid-18th century, with
a wide main street and single-storey
cottages that focus attention on the war
memorial at the far end. Aim for this and
continue out the other end of the village
towards Newton Stewart.

A former toll cottage is strategically
placed at the start of the Newton Stewart
Road and behind it an elegant 18th-century
manse. Just beyond the school is a gate
offering access to farmland and the path to
Barbellie Wood. Follow the grass path
through the field to reach a gate into the
wood – head up through the shady
woodland to reach a ladder stile over a
drystane dyke. Cross this to begin the
steep ascent of Craigengower ('Hill of
the Goats' in Gaelic) towards the
summit obelisk.

This impressive structure is a
monument to Lt Col James Hunter
Blair, mortally wounded at the Battle
of Inkerman in 1854. After the steep
ascent the views offer the perfect
excuse for a lingering break,

especially on a clear day when Ben Lomond, Arran and Ailsa Craig may be visible. From the summit, follow the wooden waymarkers south across the bleak grassy moorland before dropping down to the road north of Craig. Cross the road and take the path running roughly parallel to the river through a field, then up to the roadbridge below Craigfad. This section of path can be quite overgrown depending upon the season and recent footfall.

Turn right at the bridge along the minor road before branching right as the road turns sharp left. A grassy path leads you onwards towards Bennan Wood – take the left fork where indicated by a wooden waymarker post. This new narrower footpath dives into the woods, past clumps of primroses and violets in late spring, with the chance of spotting long-tailed tits, red squirrels, deer and badgers. At the next junction is a marker for Bennan Hill. Turn left along this, followed by a further left turn to ascend steeply via a switchback to a viewpoint overlooking Straiton. The path peters out as it reaches a field boundary;

do not cross the fence into the field, but instead turn left and the wooden platform of the viewpoint will be visible slightly downhill through the trees.

Retrace your steps to the main forest track, then turn left to continue north towards Straiton. This path eventually exits the wood onto a farm track which passes through Bennan Farm, before a footpath leaves the track/road on the right. After crossing the river via a footbridge, this returns to the car park.

◀ Colonel Hunter Blair Monument on Craigengower

53

Lady Hunter Blair's Walk

Distance 3.4km **Time** 1 hour 30
Terrain good earth footpaths and surfaced
road; no significant ascent
Map OS Landranger 77 **Access** bus from
Ayr to Straiton

**A short loop of a beautiful wooded glen
featuring dramatic waterfalls, native trees
and plenty of wildlife.**

Start at the car park at the north end of
Straiton where there is an information
board indicating a selection of walks in the
area. This walk is named after the wife of
Sir David Hunter Blair who built the
magnificent nearby Blairquhan Castle in
1820 after inheriting a tumbledown castle
and 300 acres of surrounding parkland
from his father, an Edinburgh banker.

From the car park return to the road and
turn left, then cross as indicated by the
obvious signpost. This leads through the
pretty Fowler's Croft development; the
thoughtfully designed properties which
complement the existing village
architecture won an award in 1984 for
architectural design from the Association
for the Protection of Rural Scotland. At the
end of the houses a small footpath leads to
a bridge over the Lambdoughty Burn –
cross this to reach Dalmellington Road.

Turn left along the road, crossing
Slenteuch Bridge after a short distance.
The waymarkers indicate that walkers
should take a path squeezed between the
field boundary fence and a hedge –
however, this can become heavily
overgrown and, as the path shadows the
quiet road, it is more sensible to follow the
road. A small parking area is soon reached
on the left – head into the wooded glen at
this point and take the path past a series of
attractive waterfalls, including Rossetti

◄ Lambdoughty Burn

Linn where English poet, illustrator and painter Dante Gabriel Rossetti (1828-82) was thought to have contemplated suicide.

Take the right fork at the first path junction to reach a footbridge alongside four wooden sculptures commissioned by Straiton Primary School. Ignore the footbridge for now and continue along the rough, narrowing path into the woods to view more scenic waterfalls. When the path disappears or becomes too rough, retrace your steps to the footbridge and cross. Primroses and bluebells carpet the riverbanks in late spring, and roe deer, hawks and finches may be encountered.

The earth path continues through the trees, with the choice of high route or low, as they rejoin further down the glen. You eventually reach a second footbridge, which you cross to climb back up the gorge to meet the outward path. Turn right to return to the small car park alongside Dalmellington Road.

Return to the village via the road, looking out for Largs Farm on the left 200m after the car park. This was the home of Covenanter Thomas McHaffie who was executed by dragoons in 1686 and is commemorated by a memorial in the churchyard by the west door of the church.

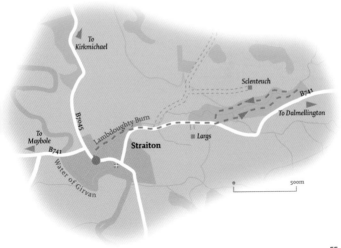

Alloway Trail

Distance 6.6km **Time** 2 hours 30
Terrain pavement, cyclepath and earth
footpaths; no significant ascent
Map OS Landranger 70 **Access** bus from
Ayr and Maybole to Alloway

A lovely circular route exploring Alloway,
birthplace of Robert Burns, and the
surrounding woodland and parks.

Park at the Burns Cottage car park on
Greenfield Avenue and cross the main road
after passing through a metal archway.
Turn right as indicated by the large black-
and-white signpost and follow the wall for
about 50m to reach the start of Poet's Path.
This walkway runs parallel to the road for
some 350m and features a series of ten
weathervanes and sculptures depicting
scenes from Robert Burns' narrative poem
Tam o' Shanter. The path curves left to reach
a wooden footbridge – cross this and the
road beyond to reach the Robert Burns
Birthplace Museum.

Turn right and walk past Alloway Parish
Church. Cross the main road to reach the
Auld Kirk, dating from 1516 and containing
the grave of Burns' father, William; it was
also the setting for the dancing witches
watched by Tam in *Tam o' Shanter*. Cross the
road again, turning right to reach the
entrance of the Burns National Monument
and Memorial Gardens. Ascend the staircase
to a walkway around the top of the
monument which gives excellent views.

After exploring the gardens, leave via the
gate at the southern end signposted 'Brig
o' Doon' and cross the lane to reach the
bridge, which was built in the 15th century
and features in the last verse of *Tam o'
Shanter* as the location where Tam's horse
Meg lost her tail in his attempt to escape
Nannie the witch.

Cross the bridge and take the path
beneath the entrance drive to Doonholm
Estate before meeting the main road. Turn
right and then left into Longhill Avenue,

◄ Tam o' Shanter weathervane

following the pavement for 200m to spy a small set of wooden steps dropping down the embankment on the other side of the road just before the roadbridge. Carefully descend these to reach a tree-lined cyclepath.

Turn right and follow this to a bridge over the River Doon. Just on the other side – before entering a tunnel – is Mungo's Well, where 'Mungo's mither hang'd hersel' in *Tam o' Shanter*. Go through the tunnel and under the B7024 to emerge beneath the wooden footbridge crossed earlier. Continue along the cyclepath and beneath another road to reach a long stretch of path skirting the eastern extremity of Alloway.

The path eventually leads via a ramp to the Maybole Road (A79) – turn left and take the first left along Kersepark and then first right into Pemberton Valley. After 250m look for a narrow lane between the houses on the right – opposite Broadwood Park – and head along this as it curves left and onto a pleasant woodland path. This easy path leads above babbling Slaphouse Burn; cross the road and re-enter the woods before reaching a path junction at the eastern corner of Rozelle Park.

Turn left and take the path through the trees to Rozelle Pavilion, turning right here to cross the open, tree-dotted parkland to

Rozelle House. Built in the 1700s this mansion and surrounding land was gifted to the people of Ayr by the Hamiltons of Rozelle in 1968.

Continue past the house to a large duck pond – only a few inches deep, so popular with ice skaters when frozen. Leave the park and turn left along the main road to reach the cluster of houses and shops that form Alloway village centre, with Burns Cottage at the far end. This two-roomed clay and thatch cottage (plus barn and byre) was built by Robert Burns' father, William Burnes, in 1757 and was the birthplace of Robert on 25 January 1759. The car park is located just past the cottage.

Maxwellston Hill

Distance 9.75km **Time** 3 hours
Terrain country lanes, earth footpaths and
faint, grassy tracks; very wet in places;
long, rough climb to the summit
Map OS Landranger 76 **Access** bus from
Ayr and Stranraer to Dailly

A tough little hill walk rewarded with
a panoramic viewpoint. Look out for
buzzards and kestrels gliding above the
open moorland.

This is one of the harder walks in the
area on which the ability to take and follow
a compass bearing would be useful should
the mist descend on the featureless
summit plateau.

Leave Dailly village square, as indicated
by the fencepost waymarker, along
Greenhead Street and The Loaning to reach
a junction by the cemetery. Cross and pass
the cemetery entrance to carry on along
the farm track towards Craig Farm with the
peat-stained waters of Lindsayston Burn
beside you. Follow the main track when it
curves right (ignoring the footpath on the
left) and continue for another 600m.

Just before reaching the farm buildings
turn sharp left to leave the farm track and
cross a ford, then go right to follow the
field boundary. After a while, this curves
left to reach a wooden stile. Cross this to
enter a patch of fairly dense gorse, with
a narrow sometimes overgrown path
weaving through the undergrowth.
After a period of wet weather this can
get boggy with gorse bushes making a
detour difficult.

The ascent remains steep as the path

emerges from the gorse adjacent to a small patch of woodland, opening out onto rough moorland terrain. Wooden waymarker posts guide you on a weaving climb to the shoulder of Hadyard Hill – the going is usually moist underfoot, but at least the gradient begins to ease. Cross a wooden stile.

Once onto the summit plateau, the wind turbines around Penwhapple Reservoir in the next valley can be seen, but the views down the Girvan Valley to the Firth of Clyde and Ailsa Craig are far more distracting. A faint path – at times an all-terrain vehicle track – between

waymarker posts leads down from Hadyard Hill and onto the final ascent to Maxwellston Hill, with its triangulation pillar atop a prehistoric fort.

This oval Pictish fort consists of two earthen ramparts above intermittent ditches and, with panoramic views, it's easy to see the defensive potential. Robert the Bruce and three hundred of his followers are also thought to have taken refuge here for three days after crossing from Arran to make an unsuccessful attack on Turnberry Castle.

Enjoy the 360-degree vista before following the outward route back to Dailly.

◄ Path on Maxwellston Hill

Dailly circular to Barony Hill

Distance 11.3km **Time** 3 hours 30
Terrain country lanes, earth footpaths and
faint, grassy tracks; very wet in places;
rough ascent to the summit
Map OS Landranger 76 **Access** bus from
Ayr and Stranraer to Dailly

A walk of contrasts – open moorland views,
a summit ridge and idyllic woodland.
There's even a ruined castle or two.

A 'Dailly Trails' board in the village
square offers a large-scale map of the route
out of the village; follow the B741 east as it
passes the church and curves right to reach
a crossroads. Cross when safe and head up
the surfaced minor road as indicated by
the metal oak leaf path marker. This metal
post will become familiar as the walk
progresses, representing the Colliers' Oak
where local mine owners used to meet
with the Laird of Dalquharran. Carry on up

the road, gradually gaining height and
enjoying views over the Girvan Valley, to
branch left as indicated by a red waymarker
arrow before the farm at Balcamie.

A rougher farm track leads between
hedgerows and across Mill Burn to meet a
minor road at Gettybeg. Cross the road onto
the access road for Whitehill Farm. Just past
the farm buildings, take the rough rocky
track continuing uphill and go through the
gate as this becomes an earth path. At the
next gate, resist the temptation to head
straight on up across the moorland to the
summit ridge; instead turn right to follow
the field boundary downhill. Pass a ruined
sheepfold and step across a small burn to
reach a set of wooden steps. Go over these
and follow a faint path through the grass
towards a wooden post by a small cairn.

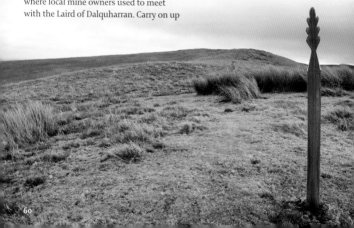

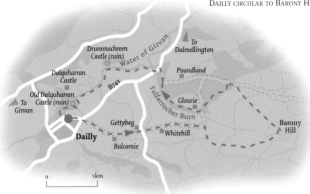

Cross the next fence via a stile and stride out across the rough moorland. Follow the wooden posts before reaching a stile immediately below the final summit ridge of Barony Hill. A narrow path follows the wooden posts, supplemented by the metal oak leaf waymarkers. Turning around, the views along the valley to the Firth of Clyde are impressive, with a wooden bench next to the triangulation pillar on the summit the perfect spot to take it all in.

The marked descent route, which can get boggy, leads to the farm track at Glengee Wood. Go through the gate to enter the woods and follow the track as it winds downhill. After about 200m, take the footpath branching left to contour through the trees with occasional glimpses of Dailly nestling in the valley below. Cross a couple of ladder stiles straddling a farm track by Glourie and enter picturesque Falfarrocher Glen, a wonderful mature woodland with a good earth path descending to a minor road. Turn left to follow this to the B741.

Go straight across this towards the metal oak leaf marker and follow a narrow path through a final patch of woodland, crossing wooden duckboards and footbridges, to join a path along the Water of Girvan. On the north bank of the river you'll see the ruins of Drummochreen Castle – a former seat of the McAlexander clan - possibly built in the late 16th century and now little more than a pile of rubble. However, the much more intact remains of Grade A-listed Dalquharran Castle can be seen on higher ground further along the river, built in 1786 to a Robert Adam design, in a similar style to Culzean Castle, and expanded in 1881.

Continue along the riverside path until you come to a green wooden bridge. Cross this to reach the ruins of the old Dalquharran Castle – built in 1679 and the former residence of the Kennedy family before the larger house further up the hill was built. Continue southwest along the riverbank before crossing back over the river at an ornate footbridge, erected in 2002. Turn left to return to the village centre.

◂ Waymarker on Barony Hill

Byne Hill above Girvan

Distance 6km Time 2 hours
Terrain **pavement, farm tracks and grassy
paths; slow, steady climb on outward route**
Map **OS Landranger 76** Access **trains from
Ayr and Stranraer to Girvan, which is also
well served by buses**

**An ascent of popular Byne Hill offering
some of the best views in the county.**

Girvan is a traditional seaside resort
whose pleasant seafront and harbour and
relaxed pace make it worth a wander.
From the car park at the south end of town
– equipped with a small takeaway booth
and public toilets – follow the Ayrshire
Coastal Path south along the good
roadside pavement, enjoying the varied
foreshore geology of Horse Rock and
Woodland Bay, all the time in the company
of Ailsa Craig offshore. Take the second
turning on the left – after the minor road
leading to Shalloch Mill and the bridge
over Myoch Burn.

Follow the farm track past a lay-by to a
gate leading to a further track heading
uphill and parallel to the A77 below. This
easy track passes through a first gate and
over a stile at a second, just above a patch
of woodland. After passing a small quarry,
the terrain steepens as the monument
comes into view ahead. Ignore any paths
branching off from the main route and
keep aiming for the monument.

The obelisk was erected in memory of
the father of a former resident of Armillan
Castle, the remains of which can be found
in the caravan park beyond the woodland
to the west of the monument. Major

Archibald Clifford Blackwell Craufurd served in India and Africa and helped to capture the Cape of Good Hope from the Dutch in 1795; sadly the once-impressive monument in his honour is in a very poor state of repair.

Continue along the track, watching out for a gate in the field boundary on the left – go through this to begin the steep ascent towards Byne Hill summit. The going is steep and rocky in places, but soon reaches a stile in the post-and-wire fence on the right. Head over this and along a narrow grassy path which soon gives way to rocky ground again. After this final loose section follow the grass path to the 214m summit – adorned with a

direction indicator and impressive views across the Firth of Clyde. On a clear day it is possible to see across to Northern Ireland, with Arran and the Mull of Kintyre closer to hand. The volcanic plug of Ailsa Craig sits about 13km offshore, formed of the blue hone granite used for curling stones. Return via the outward route – this time with Girvan and the bay in view all the way.

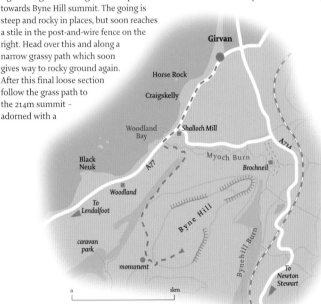

Dinmurchie Trail

Distance 5km **Time** 1 hour 30
Terrain quiet surfaced roads, farm tracks
and footpaths; boggy moorland; gradual,
winding ascent **Map** OS Landranger 76
Access no public transport to the start

**Enjoy a variety of walking terrain, from
dense mixed woodland to rolling
farmland, in this exploration of the hills
around the conservation village of Barr.**

Walkers are well provided for in Barr,
with a dedicated walkers' car park 1km
east of the village containing picnic tables
and an information board. (This circuit
could also easily be started from within
the village by following the Water of
Gregg east.)

Green waymarker arrows indicate the
route from the car park, heading downhill
and back towards the village before
turning left along a good track towards
Craigmalloch. Follow this past Changue

House and along the gurgling Water of
Gregg, and go through a gate to reach a
fork. Take the farm track on the right to
begin a gradual winding ascent. Pass
through a gate, being sure to close it
behind you, and cross a field to a stile at
the Darley Plantation boundary. Cross this
and climb the slowly rising forestry track.

Ignore a path forking left, signposted
'Fairy Knowe Trail', and continue along the
Dinmurchie Trail. The made track ends
after another 300m and an overgrown grass
track branches sharply right to the highest
point on the route at around 250m. This
path (and forest) ends abruptly at a double
stile, with beautiful views over farmland
with the Stinchar Valley and Carrick Hills
beyond. Turn right, cross another stile and
follow a ruinous drystane dyke downhill
through the moorland – some of this is
pretty boggy, but avoidable with some
weaving around.

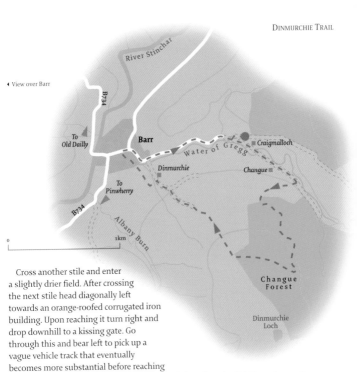

◀ View over Barr

Cross another stile and enter a slightly drier field. After crossing the next stile head diagonally left towards an orange-roofed corrugated iron building. Upon reaching it turn right and drop downhill to a kissing gate. Go through this and bear left to pick up a vague vehicle track that eventually becomes more substantial before reaching a junction just before Dinmurchie Farm.

Dinmurchie has an unlikely place in Scotland's history as the birthplace of James Dalrymple, 1st Viscount Stair; his mother unexpectedly went into labour here while visiting Barr. From such humble beginnings Dalrymple went on to become regarded as Scotland's greatest jurist and his *Institutions of the Law of Scotland*, first published in 1681, is the foundation of modern Scots law.

Turn left before reaching the farm and pass through another kissing gate on the left. Follow the field boundary and cross a stile on the right. Head diagonally right across the field towards yet another stile, cross this and turn left to descend into Barr via a minor road. Turn right at the pebbledash doctor's surgery to cross a small footbridge over the Water of Gregg and reach Changue Road opposite the 200-year-old Kings Arms Hotel. Turn right and follow the river to return to the car park – the picturesque waterside makes for a pleasant and interesting walk along this quiet stretch of road.

Changue and the Devil's Trail

Distance 7km **Time** 2 hours **Terrain** quiet surfaced roads, farm tracks, earth paths; gently undulating route with one long, tiring ascent and a steep descent
Map OS Landranger 76 **Access** no public transport to the start

A straightforward circuit of Changue Forest, offering panoramic views over the Stinchar Valley and Carrick hills.

Walkers are well provided for in the beautiful conservation village of Barr, with a dedicated walkers' car park 1km east of the village containing picnic tables and an information board. (This circuit could also easily be started from within the village by following the Water of Gregg east.)

Blue waymarker arrows indicate the route from the car park, heading downhill and back towards the village before turning left along a good track towards Craigmalloch. Follow the track as it passes Changue House whilst shadowing the gurgling Water of Gregg, and go through a gate to reach a fork. Take the track branching to the left, as indicated by a wooden signpost, and go through a gate as the glen steepens and the mixed woodland alongside the track thickens. This easy walking continues for 1km before the track crosses a bridge and begins a gentle curve to the left, passing Fairy Knowe where a short but steep detour over a wooden footbridge and up grassy steps offers a great picnic spot overlooking a waterfall.

Carry on along the main forest track to a clearing after 1km, where you branch left onto a smaller footpath signposted 'Devil's Trail' with the now familiar blue waymarker arrow. In sharp contrast to the easy walking encountered to this point,

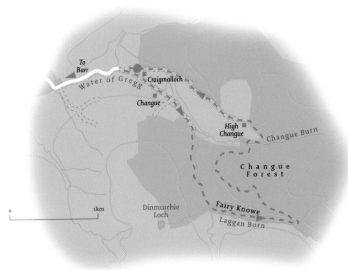

this narrow grass path climbs steeply. Surrounded by the massed ranks of a conifer plantation, the path widens slightly and the gradient then eases. Reaching a T-junction, turn left along a more substantial track and follow this for 1km to round Changue Point whilst looking out for a small path dropping down the gully on the left. This narrow, slippery path gives a steep descent to Changue Burn, a haven for primroses and bluebells in late spring. Cross a footbridge to climb back out of the valley and up a short flight of steps to meet a forestry track above High Changue.

Turn left and begin the walk back towards the car park with impressive views across the Stinchar Valley to the wild hills

beyond. The hills to the right are the site of the legend that gives this route its name. The Laird of Changue – a well-known smuggler of whisky, 'as bold and desperate as he was notorious' – struck a deal with the Devil in which he would become rich in return for his soul. For years afterwards the Laird's smuggling enterprises flourished; he always seemed to evade the excisemen and he spent freely, acquiring land and property. Eventually, however, the Devil came to collect – at which point the Laird decided he was unwilling to uphold his side of the bargain. Laying his Bible on the ground, he drew a circle around himself with his sword and with a display of impressive swordsmanship successfully defeated the Devil.

Kildoon Hill over Maybole

Distance 10km **Time** 3 hours
Terrain quiet country lanes, old coach road
and grass paths; fair amount of gradual
ascent, plus a final summit climb; steep
drops from the monument
Map OS Landranger 70 or 76
Access trains from Ayr and Stranraer to
Maybole, which is also well served by buses

A relatively straightforward circular route
from Maybole, including an ascent of local
landmark Kildoon Hill.

The walk begins from Maybole train
station opposite Town Green – cross the
road, follow the path across the green and
go down School Vennel to reach the High
Street. Turn right along the pavement and
pass the imposing Town Hall, built in 1887
as the seat of power for the old county of
Carrick. The current building contains
elements of the Tolbooth, or ancient
Prison of Maybole, and was once the
town residence of the Lairds of
Blairquhan. Continue along the High

Street and, after around 300m, fork left
along Coral Glen – not at all aquatic and, in
fact, a corruption of 'Quarry Glen' via
'Quarrle Glen' after the fireclay or 'quarl'
extracted in the area. As the road descends
and curves left look carefully on the right-
hand side of the road for the bricked-up
well known as the 'Wee Spout in the Glen'.

Continue downhill to the church of Our
Lady & St Cuthbert, then turn right and
head steeply uphill along Allan's Hill
enjoying pleasant pastoral views over the
Ayrshire countryside. The monument atop
Kildoon Hill is obvious ahead, with a
hedgerow-lined lane snaking into the
distance. Continue over the brow of the
hill and descend to a footbridge alongside
a rough ford – cross this and join a minor
road. The going is easy, with minimal
changes in elevation bar a slight incline at
the railway bridge, so simply enjoy the
walk whilst looking out for an old coach
road branching right 600m after the bridge,
signposted for Kildoon Hill.

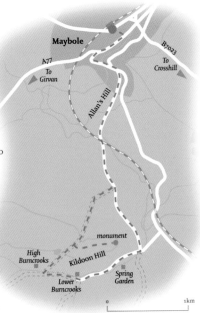

Follow the rough but well-made track through a wooded avenue as it curves left and begins to ascend to the bealach between Knockbrake and Kildoon Hill, eventually reaching a couple of wooden gates above a small lochan. Go through the kissing gate on the left adjacent to a metal five-bar gate and make your way along the ridge on one of the many sheep tracks. The tip of the monument – in memory of Sir Charles Fergusson of Kilkerran who died in 1849 – is constantly in view to aid navigation and is located within the ramparts of a prehistoric fort. The three external ramparts are clearly visible when approaching the summit along the ridge from the west, as well as the obvious entrance through the inner rampart.

Retrace your steps to the kissing gate and turn left; climb over the stile, ignoring the smaller path to the right signposted for Maybole and instead following the clear continuation of the coach road straight ahead. The path quickly becomes overgrown with gorse and is potentially muddy at the pinch-points, but soon crosses another stile and begins a steep descent alongside the remains of a drystane dyke to a wooden footbridge. Cross this bridge and scramble up the other side to a stile in the field boundary. Turn left along the quiet surfaced road to pass Lower Burncrooks on the left and ignore the minor road on the right signposted for Kirkoswald.

Follow the road for another 800m and pass Spring Garden Farm before turning left at the next road junction just before the bridge over Capenoch Burn. This road – signposted for Maybole – skirts the eastern end of Kildoon Hill and the steep rocky cliffs below the monument before rejoining the outward route to Maybole.

◀ Fergusson monument on Kildoon Hill

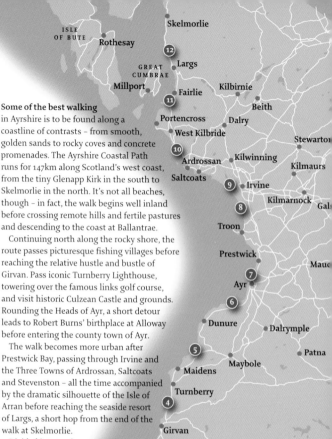

Some of the best walking
in Ayrshire is to be found along a
coastline of contrasts – from smooth,
golden sands to rocky coves and concrete
promenades. The Ayrshire Coastal Path
runs for 147km along Scotland's west coast,
from the tiny Glenapp Kirk in the south to
Skelmorlie in the north. It's not all beaches,
though – in fact, the walk begins well inland
before crossing remote hills and fertile pastures
and descending to the coast at Ballantrae.

Continuing north along the rocky shore, the
route passes picturesque fishing villages before
reaching the relative hustle and bustle of
Girvan. Pass iconic Turnberry Lighthouse,
towering over the famous links golf course,
and visit historic Culzean Castle and grounds.
Rounding the Heads of Ayr, a short detour
leads to Robert Burns' birthplace at Alloway
before entering the county town of Ayr.

The walk becomes more urban after
Prestwick Bay, passing through Irvine and
the Three Towns of Ardrossan, Saltcoats
and Stevenston – all the time accompanied
by the dramatic silhouette of the Isle of
Arran before reaching the seaside resort
of Largs, a short hop from the end of the
walk at Skelmorlie.

Divided into twelve sections
and blessed with good transport
links, the route can easily
be sampled as a series of
day walks, or tackled in
one go if you want more
of a challenge.

Ayrshire Coastal Path

Glenapp to Ballantrae

Distance 15km **Time** 4 hours 30
Terrain rough estate roads, grassy paths,
farm tracks and surfaced roads; steep
sections early on **Map** OS Landranger 76
Access buses from Ayr and Stranraer
to Girvan and Ballantrae

A pleasant country walk through the hills
and along the grassy clifftop of a
picturesque corner of South Ayrshire.

Tiny Glenapp Kirk – reputedly one of the
smallest in Scotland – sits on the opposite
side of the busy A77 to the southern
terminus of the Ayrshire Coastal Path.
With the coast still yet to be viewed, turn
your back on the kirk and head along the
estate track opposite – a gentle uphill
warm-up prior to branching right at
Craiganlea House and beginning a steeper
ascent to round the southern end of
Sandloch Hill. The coastal views begin at
this point with busy Loch Ryan below and

Corsewall Lighthouse beyond on the
northern tip of the Rhinns of Galloway.

Follow the track as it curves back inland
through the cleavage of Sandloch and
Blarbuie Hills to reach a wild moorland
plateau dotted with prehistoric earthworks
and standing stones. Continue along the
easy track, occasionally moist underfoot
after heavy rain, to bypass Glendrisaig Farm
down to the left. After a while, branch left
towards the sea, then stay on the main
track as it curves right and passes a ruined
cottage before aiming seaward high above
Shallochwreck Burn. The path descends
sharply to reach tranquil Currarie Port,
which would have been a perfect haven for
Ayrshire's 18th-century smugglers.

An estate track leads over a bridge before
rising above Currarie Glen to reach a fence
and drystane dyke leading steeply uphill to
the left. Follow this to reach a wide grassy
strip running between the steep cliffs and

seaward field boundary – walk northeast along this for 1.5km. As the grassy strip widens into livestock pasture, path-finding can be sightly problematic – thankfully large green and white reflective signs have been erected to direct walkers towards the appropriate breaks in the field boundaries.

After a series of fields, walkers are directed down to the southwest corner of Downan Hill. Skirt the seaward side of the hill onto a new farm track until this starts to curve up towards the farm buildings on the far side, then leave the track to reach a kissing gate in the far corner of the field.

Now on the surfaced road, turn left and pass through Langdale and Downan Farms to be presented with extensive views along the Ayrshire coastline. In the foreground is the 1.5km-long gravel bank at the mouth of the River Stinchar – a designated Site of Special Scientific Interest (SSSI) due to the large number of terns that choose this location for breeding during the summer months.

Carry on along the road to reach the A77 and turn left along the pavement towards the parallel bridges crossing the river. The original route crossed via the old 1776 bridge, but this is closed due to its dangerous condition, so instead use the bridge on the main road. Follow the road as it enters Ballantrae, continue to the church and turn left down The Vennel to reach a car park at the beach, adjacent to the aforementioned gravel banks.

◀ Above Ballantrae

Ballantrae to Lendalfoot

Distance 10.6km Time 4 hours
Terrain surfaced roads, sandy beaches and
grassy roadside verges; gentle ascent over
Bennane Head Map OS Landranger 76
Access buses from Ayr and Stranraer to
Ballantrae and Lendalfoot

The second stage of the Ayrshire Coastal
Path follows the sandy and rocky
shoreline and disused road before
running alongside the busy A77.

From the car park at the south end of
Ballantrae, walk north along the sandy
beach to reach the small protected harbour
at The Foreland. Dating from 1846, this was
once a thriving herring port until larger
modern fishing boats outgrew it and
herring stocks declined. A small slip leads
onto the beach – the firm sand makes this
an easy 3km with Ailsa Craig a constant
companion on the horizon as the waypoint
of Bennane Head draws nearer.

Turn inland at a burn beneath the two
cottages that form Bennane Lea to reach
the disused A77 that skirts around
Bennane Head. Pass a small cairn erected
in memory of Henry Ewing Torbert (or
'Snib') – a hermit who spent many years
living in nearby Bennane Cave until his
death in 1983 at the age of 71. The walled
cave can be explored reasonably easily and
penetrates deep into the hillside. Follow
the route gently uphill, avoiding the
livestock that may be found on the former
road, to reach a car park and viewpoint
overlooking Balcreuchan Port and Sawney
Bean's Cave – according to legend, this
was home to a family of cannibals who
devoured travellers along the Carrick
coast in the 16th century.

From the car park, the route runs
alongside the A77, with a narrow grassy
path between the fence and the seaward
side of the crash barrier. Thankfully, this

corralling ends after 1.5km at Bennane Shore Holiday Park and it is possible to either walk along the shore or the narrow asphalt pavement. A pretty group of wooden houses comes into view with the marginally larger settlement of Lendalfoot beyond, providing an almost Scandinavian scene amongst the volcanic rock outcrops.

South of Carleton Bay is a well-maintained picnic area with a magnificent bronze memorial to the Imperial Russian battle-cruiser *Varyag*, which sank 500m offshore whilst being towed south for scrap in 1920. Thanks to heroism displayed in an epic battle in the Russo-Japanese war in 1904, *Varyag* holds legendary status amongst Russians, and the unveiling of the monument was televised live throughout Russia. Passing the memorial the route continues past a row of fishermen's cottages, several tiny slips and breakwaters to reach an old black fisherman's hut almost built into the rocks. A few hundred metres landward of the A77 stand the ruins of Carleton Castle, the ancestral home of the Cathcarts, allies of the feared Kennedy family that once ruled over Carrick.

Lendalfoot offers little in the way of facilities other than a phonebox, but the regular coastal bus service stops here when hailed and allows for swift onward or return transport.

◀ Near Bennane Head

Lendalfoot to Girvan

Distance 11km **Time** 4 hours
Terrain pavements, sandy and rocky
beach, farm track and promenade; one
short sharp climb **Map** OS Landranger 76
Access buses from Ayr and Stranraer to
Lendalfoot and Girvan

This third stage of the Ayrshire Coastal
Path follows much of the sandy and rocky
shoreline with a pleasant diversion onto
a high-level coach road.

Head north along the pavement from
Lendalfoot to reach a small memorial to
the crew of a shipwrecked vessel dating
back to December 1711. Drop down onto
the beach – a mixture of sand and rocky
outcrops – and continue until you come to
Pinbain Burn. Where safe, ascend to the
roadside verge and cross where indicated,
taking extreme care on this fast road. Pass

through a kissing gate to climb uphill on
an old coach road – the only road along
this section of coast prior to the advent of
motorised vehicles. Judging by the slope
aspect this can't have been an entirely
pleasant experience for the coach horses,
but the scenery offers ample justification
for walkers to take frequent breaks.

Once atop the main coach road, pay
attention to the remnants of surfaced road
beneath your feet – this is an early
example of the macadamised construction
technique developed by local boy John
Loudon McAdam in the late-18th century.
Prior to the descent towards Ardwell Bay,
bypass a roadside cottage, now
commandeered as a sheep pen, on the
seaward side, before following the track
down towards a series of muddy fields.
Follow the boggy path north (ignoring

a continuation of the path to the main road), leaving the track to avoid the worst of the muddy patches. Pass through the final kissing gate before the farm and cross back over the main A77 road when safe.

Drop down to the beach or continue along the roadside verge where appropriate, though be aware of a nasty pathless section on a blind bend where the beach is a far better option. Enjoy the varied textures and geology of Black Neuk, Woodland Bay and Horse Rock before heading up to the car park and toilets at the southern end of Girvan promenade.

Continue along this pleasant surfaced path adjacent to Stair Park before bearing right after the boating lake to reach the newer car park at the harbour.

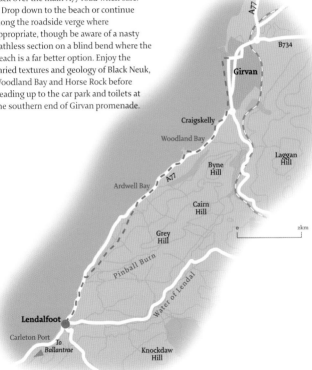

◀ North of Lendalfoot

Girvan to Maidens

Distance 13.6km **Time** 4 hours
Terrain pavements and minor roads,
sandy and rocky beach and farm track; no
significant ascent **Map** OS Landranger 76
Access buses from Ayr and Stranraer to
Girvan and Maidens

This stage of the Ayrshire Coastal Path
runs along the shoreline of rocks and sand
before cutting across the world-famous
Turnberry Golf Course.

From the harbour, keep the river on your
left and head towards Girvan town centre.
At the traffic lights, turn left along the
pavement and then left again, following
the brown campsite sign. Cross the bridge
over the River Girvan and turn left, passing
Noble's Shipyard – one of the last
remaining shipyards on the Clyde.
Continue past the Coastguard Station

before reaching the redeveloped former
coal terminal, landscaped by the local
Rotary Club. Press on along the path as it
opens out at a small green before the
municipal golf course. Turn right through
the car park and pass between the row of
terraced houses beyond to arrive at a minor
road above the river.

Go left here and enjoy the easy walking
along this quiet road as it bisects the golf
course before coming to a T-junction. Head
left to reach Girvan Mains Farm, adjacent
to the faint outline of a Roman Camp. The
route passes through the busy farm and
onto a track aiming seaward which passes
Gallow Hill – a reminder of the harsh
punishments doled out by the ruling
Kennedy clan in times past. The track
swings north on reaching the coast,
passing fields where the unsurpassed

◄ Girvan shoreline

Ayrshire potatoes are grown in the sandy soil. Carry on along the grassy foreshore to reach a couple of cottages at Curragh.

Drop down to the sand and shingle beach and cross the mouth of Dipple Burn via a concrete causeway constructed below the alginate factory. Beyond this point the beach becomes predominantly shingle, and it is far easier to walk along the grassy verge beneath the field boundary fence. This also ensures that ringed plovers and oystercatchers nesting in the shingle are avoided. Soon the firm sand returns, making for easy walking, before you cross Milton Burn via another causeway and emerge onto the broad golden sweep of Turnberry Bay.

With Turnberry Lighthouse in view on the headland in front of you, amble along this pleasant beach until a path heads up the escarpment and onto Turnberry Golf Course. Taking great care not to disturb the golfers attempting holes, including the infamous 9th known as Bruce's Castle, follow the path between the fairways to cross the wartime RAF Turnberry runway and arrive at a gate alongside the A719. Turn left along a roadside pavement to gently drop down into Maidens.

Note that during major golf tournaments the last section of this walk may well be closed, in which case walkers will be required to head up a path alongside Milton Burn and turn left to follow the A719 into Maidens.

Maidens to Dunure

Distance 11km **Time** 4 hours 30
Terrain sandy and rocky beaches, farm
tracks, surfaced roads; gently undulating
Map OS Landranger 70 **Access** buses from
Ayr and Stranraer to Maidens and Dunure
and from Ayr to Dunure only

A walk of contrasts, from the fine roads
and tracks of Culzean Country Park to
expansive golden beaches and rocky
shoreline scrambles. It is essential to
check tide times before reaching
Croyburnfoot – a high spring tide will
require a bit of a wait or a tricky scramble.

Head north from the car park which
overlooks the drying harbour nestling in
the southern corner of Maidenhead Bay,
and drop down onto the firm sand where
appropriate. Upon reaching Hogston Burn
at the north of the bay, turn inland and
cross at a footbridge. Signs indicate that

the path is now entering National Trust for
Scotland-owned Culzean Country Park
(look out for the donations box); proceed
along the accurately named Long Avenue
to reach Swan Pond with associated car
park and visitor facilities. From this point it
is possible to take a multitude of paths to
arrive at the main castle – take a look at the
many maps and signposts to ensure
eventual arrival at the steps leading down
to the Gas House.

To continue on the Long Avenue, pass
the Walled Garden before arriving at a large
car park beside the Deer Park with its
resident herd of red deer. Beyond the car
park branch left to dip underneath a bridge
and arrive at the descent route towards the
Gas House and onward route across
Culzean Bay. The grandeur of Culzean
Castle will no doubt prove an irresistible
draw, so this would be a good point to

explore the visitor centre and surrounding buildings before descending along the path to the Gas House sheltered at the bottom of the brae.

Strike out along a path skirting the trees (or just head straight across the beach), over a rocky outcrop and onwards along 2km of firm sand to the holiday park at Croyburnfoot. Rounding the point of Isle Port will be difficult, if not impossible, at times of extreme high tide, so the relevant tidal knowledge will prevent a lengthy delay or difficult scramble. Once safely around the rocky outcrop the beach material becomes less pleasant underfoot, but this is short-lived as the path soon zigzags uphill to pass the Protected Ancient Monument of Katie Gray's Rocks – once an ancient settlement but now, as the name suggests, little more than a scattering of rocks.

Reaching the top of the cliff, the path skirts a series of fields before diving inland to cross a burn at a set of stepping stones. Continue to follow the path around the farmland to emerge at a minor road beneath a

telecommunications mast – turn left and then almost immediately left again to descend along a rough track through scrub towards Dunure, arriving via the green fields of Kennedy Park.

Dunure to Ayr

Distance 12.4km **Time** 5 hours
Terrain sandy and rocky beaches, muddy
and grassy farm tracks, promenade; some
short climbs **Map** OS Landranger 70
Access buses from Ayr and Stranraer to
Maidens and Dunure and from Ayr to
Dunure; Ayr has a train station with
regular connections to Glasgow and is
well served by buses

A tricky section of the Ayrshire Coastal
Path, featuring some rocky and slippery
foreshore, though beautiful tiny harbours
and panoramic coastal views reward the
intrepid walker. It is essential to check
tide times before leaving Dunure Harbour
- a high spring tide will necessitate a bit of
a wait or a scramble.

After leaving Kennedy Park spend
some time exploring the ruins of
Dunure Castle, the main Kennedy
stronghold in the 16th century –
though dating from far earlier. Past
the castle is a nicely intact doocote;
follow the path beyond this down
into the main village and harbour.
Improved by the Earl of Cassillis
in the 19th century, the harbour
was home to a large fishing fleet
which declined in the 20th
century to leave it the preserve

of leisure craft and the odd solo fisherman.
Circle around the harbour (checking the
state of the tide against the harbour
ladders as indicated on the sign) and drop
down onto the sandy beach beyond.

Follow the beach, weaving around, over
and through the rocky outcrops. The
standard waymarker posts are replaced
with white circles and crosses painted on
the rocks for this stage – the cattle which
graze this area are a bit too rough with the
man-made scratching posts, apparently.
The path occasionally cuts through grazing
land – again directed by white spots on

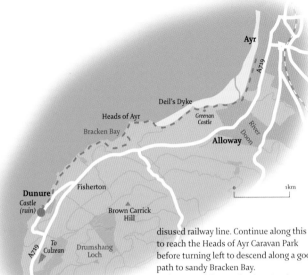

rocks – after one such inland excursion climb over a stile in a stone dyke. Continue at this higher level for 300m before descending a muddy gully to rejoin the beach. The going is tougher for a few hundred metres as the route crosses a patch of slippery rocks before rounding the headland into Fisherton Bay. However, a tidal miscalculation will prevent you from proceeding much further – the only option is to retreat or wait.

Once in Fisherton Bay the firm sand and shingle make walking easier, before a set of rough steps leads up a rocky outcrop. Follow this to emerge on a clifftop path which soon joins an easy footpath along a disused railway line. Continue along this to reach the Heads of Ayr Caravan Park before turning left to descend along a good path to sandy Bracken Bay.

Skirt round the Heads of Ayr (again, assuming tidal conditions are favourable) and carry on to reach a sandy bay beneath a holiday park, formerly part of the Butlins empire. Press on and squeeze through a rocky gap inland of the volcanic sill of Deil's Dyke to be presented with an impressive view of ruined Greenan Castle perched precariously above the bay. It is possible to detour to Robert Burns' birthplace of Alloway via the NCN 7 cycle route here. Otherwise, make the most of the relatively isolated beach for another 1km before proceeding inland to cross the footbridge over the River Doon and onto the cycleway and promenade at Seafield. Amble along the surfaced track for 1km to reach a car park overlooking the beach.

◀ Dunure Castle

Ayr to Troon

Distance 15.7km **Time** 5 hours
Terrain sandy beaches, earth track,
promenades and pavements; no
significant ascent **Map** OS Landranger 70
Access Ayr and Troon have train stations
with regular connections to Glasgow and
are well served by buses

North of Ayr, the Ayrshire Coastal Path
becomes increasingly busy as the
farmland and rolling Carrick Hills give
way to seaside resorts and industrial
endeavour. This section leaves the historic
port and county town of Ayr to follow
wide sandy bays past the airport at
Prestwick to the ferry terminal at Troon.

Leave the car park, initially following the
NCN7 cyclepath before soon crossing Low
Green via a red path to reach Georgian
Wellington Square at the imposing County
Court building. Pass the pillared entrance
and head along Cassilis Street and then
Bruce Crescent to reach the remaining
tower of St John's Church. As well as
Cromwellian musket-ball dents in the
lower tower walls, the church has a
fascinating history and it is worth
spending a little time reading the
information boards in the area. Leave the
tower on your left to carry on along
Montgomerie Terrace and rejoin the NCN7
cyclepath. Obvious signs direct walkers

(and cyclists) along the walls of the former bastion to Loudoun Hall, a 15th-century townhouse and the oldest building in Ayr.

Cross the New Bridge to remain on the NCN7 route along Main Street, and follow the waymarking through a succession of industrial backroads before crossing a final bridge to arrive at Newton-on-Ayr promenade. Follow this to reach a rough track running seaward of a golf course, before diving left down a ramp to the beach. Round Bentfield Point and hop up to the promenade to arrive in Prestwick. Follow the promenade for 2km before reaching a children's playground within the former public swimming pool. Continue onwards as the path drops down to the sandy beach, and watch out for a large pole indicating a path heading inland through the dunes before the Pow Burn. Cross the golf course practice ground to shadow the Pow Burn and cross a footbridge towards a holiday park. Skirt around this to rejoin the beach on the northern side of the burn.

Now on Troon South Sands below the Royal Troon Golf Course, continue along the pleasant beach until you reach the promenade which you can now follow if you wish. At the northern end of the bay a path leads up onto a long grassy mound on the southwestern side of the promontory that protects Troon Harbour. Enjoy the views from atop Ballast Bank – formed from the discarded ballast of coal ships prior to loading in the harbour below. Drop from the end of the bank and follow the minor road back inland past the lifeboat station, sawmill and industrial units to reach the marina with large car park.

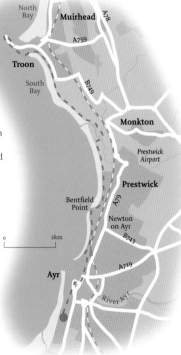

Troon to Irvine

Distance 11km **Time** 3 hours 30
Terrain sandy beach, tracks and pavement;
no significant ascent **Map** OS Landranger 70
Access Troon and Irvine both have train
stations with regular connections to
Glasgow and are well served by buses

**An easy section following the promenade
out of Troon before a stroll along sandy
Irvine Bay and into Irvine Harbour
overlooking Bogside Flats.**

Passing the entrance to the P&O Ferry
Terminal, rejoin the familiar NCN7
cyclepath for a short distance as it threads
a pleasant route around North Bay. Leave

the cyclepath as it heads inland at Barassie
and continue along the grass foreshore
before dropping down onto the firm sand.
Continue along the beach below the links
golf courses of Barassie, Western Gailes
and Glasgow Gailes as far as a large marker
post in the dunes. It is possible to continue
along the beach from this point all the way
to the mouth of the River Irvine, but for a
bit of variety (or an escape from the wind)
head inland at this point.

This path, at the northern end of the
Western Gailes golf course, runs parallel to
the beach but behind the tall dunes,
offering shelter from an onshore wind.

After passing a few stands of pine tree the path emerges at Irvine Beach Park, built on reclaimed land and landscaped with ponds and paths. Cross this via a route of your choice to arrive at the Bridge of Scottish Invention, the pedestrian access to the sadly closed Big Idea Inventor Centre across the river. Until the museum site is redeveloped this bridge will remain closed, so the Ayrshire Coastal Path currently continues inland from this point.

Again on the NCN7 cyclepath head towards Irvine railway station, passing along Irvine Harbour – Glasgow's seaport until Port Glasgow was constructed in the late 17th century. The Scottish Maritime Museum has moored many historic vessels alongside the old harbour jetties, and the estuary also provides shelter to a number of pleasurecraft on moorings. Leaving the harbour behind the railway station comes into view ahead – ignore this and turn left to follow the cycleway to a roundabout. Turn right and head under the railway bridge, then past a small church on the left. Continue parallel to the road before dipping through an underpass to emerge alongside the River Irvine again. Cross the footbridge to reach Low Green and the town beyond.

◀ Dragon sculpture, Irvine

Irvine to Ardrossan

Distance 14.8km **Time** 4 hours 30
Terrain surfaced roads and cyclepaths,
promenades and sandy beaches; no
significant ascent **Map** OS Landranger 70
Access Irvine and Ardrossan both have
train stations with regular connections to
Glasgow and are well served by buses

A fairly industrial section of the Ayrshire
Coastal Path leaves Irvine to pass through
'The Three Towns' of Stevenston,
Saltcoats and Ardrossan. The route
follows the National Cycle Network
Routes 7 and 73 for much of the way.

The route is well-waymarked with the
Ayrshire Coastal Path logo featuring on
many of the NCN7 signs. On a surfaced
cyclepath head north along the River
Irvine, under the roadbridge and on
towards a prominent Robert Burns statue.

Soon the common ground of Towns Moor
will be reached, featuring the oval track of
Cadgers' Racecourse where carthorses and
ponies are still raced in mid August. Now
following the route of the railway, cross a
minor road and continue along the
cyclepath before branching right where
indicated and shadowing the quiet B779
north. Garnock Floods Wildlife Reserve is
on the left, providing a wetland habitat for
ducks, geese and waders.

Immediately after crossing the bridge
turn sharp right to proceed through a
short stretch of woodland and under the
A78(T) via a tunnel to rejoin a riverside
path. Follow this as it curves left, then
ignoring a footbridge on the right and a
signed path towards Kilwinning, proceed
along the NCN73 westwards towards
Ardrossan. The path runs through an

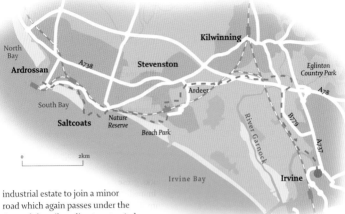

industrial estate to join a minor road which again passes under the A78 and the railway line to enter Ardeer Park after 2.75km of easy walking.

Upon reaching New Street in Stevenston, turn left towards the railway station, cross the level crossing and continue along the pavement (ignoring the NCN73 bearing right) until an Ayrshire Coastal Path signpost indicates a right turn towards Stevenston Beach Park. Bear right and pass through the car park to reach a new footbridge over Stevenston Burn and cross this to reach the sandy beach. From here, it is possible to bear sharp right across the dunes to regain the NCN73 alongside the railway, or continue onwards to walk along the beach, trending right. Head up the ramp at the western end of the beach to reach a long promenade stretching all the way to Saltcoats Harbour.

The name 'Saltcoats' or 'Saltcottis' is derived from ancient times when salt was extracted from seawater in the area – the 'cottis' being the local dwellings. In more

modern times Saltcoats Harbour was a key port in the export of coal until the completion of the deep-water harbour at Ardrossan in the early 19th century. The Victorian love of coastal resorts led to a brief resurgence in popularity towards the end of the century, indicated by the impressive villas lining the seafront, but the rise of cheap overseas holidays has seen Saltcoats decline somewhat over recent years.

Continue along the promenade or golden sands of South Beach until Saltcoats seamlessly blends into Ardrossan as Stanley Burn emerges from the seawall. Cross the level crossing at Ardrossan Town Station and continue along wide Princes Street. Cross the main road to arrive at Clyde Marina, part of a regeneration scheme surrounded by modern luxury apartments.

Ardrossan to Portencross

Distance 10.5km **Time** 3 hours 30
Terrain surfaced roads and cyclepaths,
promenades and sandy beaches; no
significant ascent **Map** OS Landranger 63
Access Ardrossan has a train station with
regular connections to Glasgow and is
well served by buses; Portencross has no
public transport, so requires a 2km walk
from the nearest station at West Kilbride

Leaving the industrial Three Towns
behind, this section of the route rejoins
the relative tranquillity of the sandy shore
beneath farmland and the Craft Town of
West Kilbride.

From Ardrossan Town Station, turn
right to circle around Clyde Marina – a
regenerative development in the former
19th-century coal port. Passing the
harbourmaster tower the low outline of
Horse Isle is visible beyond the outer
breakwater, surmounted by a tall beacon

erected by the Earl of Eglinton in 1811. The
next basin was formerly used by tankers
discharging at the former Shell oil
terminal. There are plans to redevelop this
area to accommodate a further 360-berth
marina, but for the time being the path
winds along a slightly precarious path
around the derelict facility.

Now in North Bay walkers can choose to
follow the beach or the asphalt path
alongside the road (or a combination of
the two). The route is obvious, allowing
attention to drift towards the jagged
skyline of Arran on the horizon and the
scenic sandy beach penetrated by igneous
dykes stretching for several kilometres
ahead. Entering Seamill, a footbridge
across the Kilbride Burn offers views
towards the original 18th-century Sea Mill
from which the settlement takes its name.
Continue along the beach beneath Seamill
Hydro Hotel, a former hydropathic spa that

now houses extensive conference and leisure facilities and occasionally hosts the Scotland football team.

A small car park signals an escape route for walkers up to the village and A78; otherwise continue along a well-made path between the golf course and beach – often well populated with joggers from the dormitory town of West Kilbride. Stay on the path along Ardneil Bay to round Farland Head, with the Iron Age fort and dun coming into view atop Auld Hill.

The path peters out here, necessitating a brief walk across the shingle to reach a kissing gate in the field boundary ahead. Go through this and cross the potentially boggy field, sometimes with livestock, to arrive at Portencross car park.

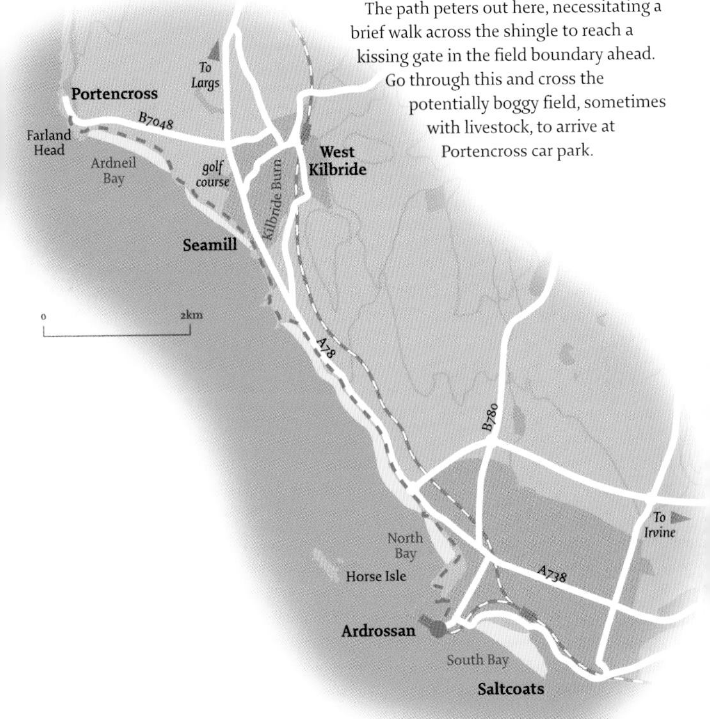

Portencross
Farland Head
B7048
Ardneil Bay
golf course
Seamill
West Kilbride
Kilbride Burn
To Largs
A78
To Irvine
B780
North Bay
Horse Isle
A738
Ardrossan
South Bay
Saltcoats
0   2km

◀ Arran from the shore

Portencross to Largs Marina

Distance 11.5km **Time** 4 hours
Terrain surfaced roads and cyclepaths,
promenades and farm tracks; no
significant ascent **Map** OS Landranger 63
Access Portencross has no public
transport, so requires a 2km walk from
West Kilbride; Largs has a train station
with regular connections to Glasgow and
is well served by buses

**Good trails lead along the shore from
Portencross before skirting beneath the
hulk of Hunterston Power Station which
dominates this area. It then leads on to
the huge marina south of Largs.**

Leave Portencross car park to bear north
on the minor road as directed, passing the
houses before leaving the road to reach the
well-preserved peel tower of Portencross
Castle, built in the 14th century and
occupied until 1739 when a storm damaged
the roof. The castle has a fascinating
history – located halfway between
Dundonald and Rothesay, King Robert II
was a frequent visitor. The tiny harbour
beneath the tower still houses a few boats

in the summer, replacing the small fishing
fleet that was once protected here.

Follow the farm track north with views
across to Little Cumbrae and Millport
beyond, past a modern concrete pier and
into farmland beneath the sandstone cliffs
of Ardneil Hill. Before long the towering
rock is replaced by towering glass in the
form of decommissioned Hunterston A
Power Station, and the route leads along
pavement between the silent reactor
building and a construction worker
compound. Further back from the road is
the more modern Hunterston B Power
Station, currently capable of supplying
electricity to over 1.5 million homes.

The public access road continues
alongside Hunterston Sands and past the
now derelict oil rig construction yard that
failed to live up to expectations after
consuming millions of pounds of public
money. The adjacent former ore terminal
sits astride Southannan Sands – an
important winter feeding ground for

waders and seabirds – and now unloads coal via a huge conveyor to the railway line further inland. Leave the access road by branching left onto the former construction yard road before reaching a pavement alongside the A78.

Turn left along this, and enjoy 2.5km of easy walking along a surprisingly pleasant cycle track that threads through areas of woodland before arriving at a small waterside picnic area at Burnfoot. Cross the footbridge and continue along the footpath beneath the seawall as the sea view properties of well-to-do Fairlie are passed. Turn inland at Bay Street to reach the parish church, then turn left along the pavement to reach the entrance to Kelburn Country Park, estate of the Earl of Glasgow since the 13th century. In 2007 the Boyle family, ancestors of the first Earl, allowed a team of Brazilian graffiti artists to adorn the walls of Kelburn Castle with colourful murals.

Cross the road opposite the park entrance to enter a cycle and footpath leading through a tunnel beneath the railway and continuing along a path between the railway and marina boundary fence. The path verges are decorated with a collection of anchors, loaned by the now closed NATO base at Fairlie Quay. After passing the multitude of yachts in the marina the path emerges at a car park outside the marina entrance, providing the option of an onward journey by foot north into Largs or by bus from the nearby road.

◄ Portencross Castle

Largs Marina to Skelmorlie

Distance 16.5km (high); 12.6km (low)
Time 5 hours (high); 4 hours (low)
Terrain a mixture of metalled roads, beaten earth and grassy paths; the Low Route is gently undulating; the High Route is very boggy in places with more ascent – especially on Knock Hill detour
Map OS Explorer 341 **Access** Largs and Wemyss Bay have train stations with regular connections to Glasgow and are well served by buses; buses from Greenock to Skelmorlie

There are two options for this final section of the Ayrshire Coastal Path, a superb higher-level route incorporating Knock Hill and spectacular views over Largs and the Firth of Clyde or a low-level route along pleasant minor roads.

Leaving the marina pass The Pencil Monument commemorating the Battle of Largs in 1263 which finally expelled the Vikings from western Scotland. Continue along the promenade past the Cumbrae ferry terminal, the RNLI lifeboat station and Vikingar on the right, before reaching the Noddsdale Water and turning inland to reach the A78.

From this point the path splits into High and Low Routes; if taking the Low Route, cross the road, turn left and then right to follow quiet Routenburn Road uphill, passing the privately owned Knock Castle and Routenburn Golf Course whilst marvelling at the great views across the Clyde; the high route rejoins from the right.

To take the high route from the branch point in Largs, cross the road, turn right and then left to enter Barr Crescent. As soon as possible take the footpath on the left running alongside the Noddsdale – this is waymarked – and follow it until

◀ The Pencil Monument

you come to Brisbane Glen Road. Turn left and follow the road, initially on pavement but soon on the tarmac. Take the waymarked track to Brisbane Mains Farm on the left. Pass through the farmyard and along the muddy track.

As the angle of ascent increases the path becomes less defined and more boggy. Take the left (waymarked) fork at the end of a small copse to bear northwest along an open grassy track. At another fork the route of the Ayrshire Coastal Path continues ahead, though you can detour along the main track on the left to climb to the summit of Knock Hill before returning to this point. The detour gives superb views of the Cumbrae islands and the Firth of Clyde.

Back on the main route, begin the descent towards Blackhouse Burn; the path leads through potentially muddy farmland. Ignore a path branching off to the left to enter a small wooded area where leaf litter creates a pleasing cushion underfoot. The path emerges at a minor road junction by Manor Park Hotel; at this point the Low Route is rejoined – turn right along the road. Continue along this for a further 2km before descending steeply to reach Meigle and the A78.

Cross the road carefully, turn right and after 150m of hair-raising traffic interaction cross back over to head up the minor road towards Skelmorlie Castle. This climbs steeply to reach the ancestral seat of the

Montgomeries before flattening out and continuing northwards for a further 1km.

Upon reaching Skelmorlie the path begins a descent through the extremely pleasant village to reach Wemyss Bay and the bridge over the Kelly Burn, the Ayrshire-Renfrew boundary and the end of the Ayrshire Coastal Path.

Index